CLASSIC BEER STYI 4

D0331958

MÄRZEN · OKTOBERFEST
VIENNA

GEORGE & LAURIE FIX

A Brewers Publications Book

Vienna, Märzen, Oktoberfest
By George and Laurie Fix
Classic Beer Style Series
Edited by Dan Fink
Copyright 1991 by George and Laurie Fix

ISBN: 0-937381-27-6
Printed in the United States of America
10 9 8 7 6 5 4

Published by Brewers Publications,
a division of the Association of Brewers.
PO Box 1679, Boulder, Colorado 80306-1679 USA
(303) 447-0816 • FAX: (303) 447-2825

Direct all inquiries/orders to the above address.

Cover design by Robert L. Schram
Cover photography by Michael Lichter, Michael Lichter Photography
Art direction by Steve Harley

Table of Contents

Chapter 4: Practical Tips on Brewing

Acknowledgements

The authors wish to express their gratitude to Charlie Olchowski for his assistance in verifying many of the historical references used in this book.

About the Authors

Laurie and George Fix reside in Arlington, Texas, where they have lived for the past five and a half years. Laurie is a native of Western Pennsylvania and George a native Texan.

Laurie enjoys her business career as an executive secretary, with her spare time dedicated to preparing gourmet meals, browsing through her collection of over 300 cookbooks and oil painting. Laurie has participated in numerous brewing conferences and has acted as a judge in many competitions.

George earned his doctorate from Harvard University and has been on the faculty at Harvard, the University of Michigan and Carnegie-Mellon University. Currently he is chairman of the department of mathematics at the University of Texas at Arlington.

George has won 60 brewing awards, including two best-of-shows in AHA and HWBTA sanctioned competitions.

Introduction

In the simplest definition, Viennas are amber-colored beers brewed with bottom-fermenting lager yeast. On the other hand, the terms Märzen and Oktoberfest originally referred to a brewing process, not a beer style. Beer was brewed in March, stored in caves during the summer months and then served in October when cool weather returned. While the terms Vienna, Märzen and Oktoberfest may seem unrelated, historical records (reference 26) indicate that specially formulated amber lagers, most notably those with a "Viennese character," did particularly well with this extended brewing process. In fact, the origins of modern October festivals can be clearly traced back to celebrations relating to the introduction of the season's new beer in this style. Changes in technology, most notably refrigeration, made brewing year-round possible. At this point a bifurcation of the Vienna and the Märzen/Oktoberfest styles started. The former usually became standard beers brewed on a regular basis and often at a lower gravity. The Märzen and Oktoberfest beers became "festbiers" brewed for the celebrations each October. Historical records, nevertheless, indicate that successful versions of both styles had a definite

"Viennese character," and it is the primary goal of this book to delineate the fundamental attributes of the Vienna character.

This is done, first of all, with a qualitative approach in Chapter 2. Various descriptors of the desired flavor profile are given as well as a general discussion of the type of brewing ingredients that are appropriate. It is hoped that this chapter will be of interest not only to hands-on brewers, but also to those whose primary interest is in beer styles and beer evaluation. The next two chapters take a quantitative approach, and contain specific recipes as well as practical brewing tips on how to produce beers with a Vienna character. The final chapter contains a selected but representative survey of commercial examples currently available.

The monograph opens with a brief history of the style. This is of independent interest since there is no other beer style that has had such a roller-coaster trip through time, vacillating between widespread popularity and obscurity.

The bulk of the time spent preparing the material in the monograph was with the recipes. The goal was to get formulations that were on the one hand authentic and on the other hand accessible to small scale brewers. The starting point was compiling a list of formulations, including some of the authors' own, that won in AHA National Competitions. From this list, formulations were culled which seemed inappropriate in one sense or the other. The authors personally brewed at least two batches of the remaining recipes and eliminated some additional formulations on the basis of these test batches. The recipes that remained were then brewed and entered in AHA-sanctioned competitions. The ones that emerged from this fray with the best results are included in Chapter 3.

One major conflict did emerge from the background work on recipes. It is abundantly clear from historical

Oktoberfest celebration in Munich. Photo courtesy of the German National Tourist office.

references that one major feature of the traditional Viennese character was uncompromising standards in brewing ingredients. Certainly, beers in this style should be brewed in strict compliance with the Reinheitsgebot (using barley malt, yeast, hops and water only), but this by itself is not enough. Only selected barley and hop varieties were deemed suitable. In terms of modern brewing, standards like these would rule out malt made from the majority of two-row barley varieties, absolutely all six-row barley malts, concentrated wort solutions (syrups or dried malt) and most hop varieties. The problem is that these are the types of brewing ingredients that are the most readily available today to small-scale brewers. Hence, many will find criteria like these impractical. The authors are sympathetic to this viewpoint, and the original intent was to be diplomatic and somewhat neutral with respect to recommendations. A careful analysis of results from a rather large number of competitions changed the picture. "Authenticity" and "tradition" aside, there is absolutely no doubt that traditional ingredients will produce the best Vienna-style beers, and usually by a good margin. The rather strongly worded recommendations in Chapters 2 and 3 reflect this.

The recommendations, however, should be suitably interpreted. They are not meant to imply that "inferior brewing materials" are incapable of making good beer, but "good" may not be good enough. Direct brewing experience has shown that even better beer in the Viennese style results from the use of traditional ingredients. In addition, use of the latter is no guarantee of excellent beer. Defective yeast and other technical errors in brewing can nullify the desirable effects of top quality malt and hops.

In the end, individual brewers will want to use their own opinions about these matters. The traditional ingredients recommended do cost more than other alternatives, and this, particularly in commercial brewing, could be an important point. Availability and related practical issues could also favor substitutes. Nevertheless, the authors strongly urge brewers to try at least one or two batches with the recommended ingredients. There is no better way to ascertain the relevance of these points in the context of one's own brewing environment!

1

History

BREWING IN THE AUSTRO-HUNGARIAN EMPIRE

In the period prior to the 17th century, the development of Viennese brewing was similar to the development of brewing in the rest of Europe. At this time brewing was entirely in the domain of monasteries. In the 17th century brewing was passed on to the royal courts, who established a monopoly. Officers of the crown served as brewers, but they were prohibited from selling their product to the general public. Little is known about the type of beer that was produced during this period except that it was dark with a definite sweet finish, and produced with top-fermenting yeast. However, given the ease and speed with which these beers gave way to the new styles that emerged in the 19th century, their overall quality was probably poor.

Major changes started as early as the 17th century. The industrial revolution took place, and with it restrictive conditions on commercial brewing, like those cited above. In addition, this period saw the emergence of the Austro-Hungarian empire with Vienna its commercial and cultural center. It is important to note that this empire included not only what are today called Austria and Hungary, but also all of Bohemia as well. One consequence of Vienna's position in the empire is that the development of brewing in Vienna closely parallels that in Bohemia, most notably Pilsen, and the interconnections during that period were much closer than many today realize.

Of all the people that contributed to the development of brewing in the Austro-Hungarian empire, none rival the Dreher family. Their participation in commercial brewing has been traced back to the 1630s. Though many members of the family contributed to brewing, the most important member was Anton Dreher, now regarded as one of the giants of European brewing during the 19th century. He sharpened his command of brewing practice by studying his trade in various Munich breweries during the 1830s. It was there he met another major figure of 19th century brewing, Gabriel Sedlmayr. Their collaboration and friendship had major significance. In fact, it is entirely fair to say that lager brewing as we know it today would not have been possible without their achievements in brewing science, brewing technology and brewing management.

On the scientific front, it is now generally recognized that both Dreher and Sedlmayr jointly discovered that yeast was the "secret ingredient" in Bavarian monastery brewing. In the past there has been some controversy about whether Munich or Vienna was the first city to brew lager beer commercially (reference 17, pages 189 to 190). However, the most likely scenario was a collaboration. In 1841 Dreher introduced the bottom-fermenting strain in his family's brewery in Vienna, while Sedlmayr did the same at Munich. The success of this change was instantaneous, and news spread quickly. For instance, as Dave Miller points out in his monograph on Pilsener beer (reference 10), the new yeast was brought to Pilsen scarcely a year later, in 1842.

The Dreher family became known as brewers around 1632, and two centuries later Anton Dreher made some important contributions to brewing in Vienna. Photo from *One Hundred Years of Brewing*.

During the next 20 years, Dreher perfected the commercial application of the "Märzen and Oktoberfest" brewing process whereby beer was made in the spring and stored in cold cellars during the summer. Dreher's beers were very successful, and by 1860 demand had increased to the point where his brewery in Vienna was producing 20 times its 1830s volume. Demand remained strong. Dreher responded by opening a new brewery at Michalovce in Bohemia in 1867 and another in Budapest a few years later. This of course was the period when the popularity of pale Pilsener beer was growing, but the commercial acceptance of the

Vienna and Märzen/Oktoberfest, at this point identical styles, was equally strong.

Sedlmayr's operations in Munich were equally success-ful. Here the specialty was very dark beer, commonly called Münchner, which was acclaimed throughout the world. In spite of this, Bavarian brewers were keenly aware of the striking success of the new Pilsener style. Many tried ver-sions of this style, but all were apparently disappointing. Dave Miller (reference 10) pinpointed the reason for this: deficiencies in brewing science of that time. In particular, the importance of pH in wort production and how it is affected by grain and water constituent reactions was poorly understood. As a consequence, the inevitable failure of formulations using pale malts and untreated alkaline water, typical of water in Bavaria, was not anticipated.

Dreher's formulation was another matter. Like the pale beer brewed in Pilsen, it was brewed from quality Moravian barley. Many like Sedlmayr saw this barley as the real force behind the Pilsener revolution. Dreher's Vienna malts had a deeper color than that used in Pilsen but were lighter in color than Munich malts, so beers brewed with Vienna malt offered consumers a genuine alternative to Münchners. Of greatest importance is the fact that the extra acidity found in Vienna malts, not present in pale malts, and the alkaline Bavarian water was in effect a "marriage made in heaven." The beers produced were an instant success, and soon were brewed in other areas of Bavaria like Kulmbach. Happily, the same is true today!

Neither Dreher nor Sedlmayr was satisfied with the restrictions that climate and the seasons placed on brewing, and both were alert to new ideas which would give brewers control over temperature, a point of fundamental impor-tance to lager brewing. The scientific principles underlying refrigeration were understood by the mid-19th century, but lacking was what is called today "technology transfer," i.e., the conversion of fundamental ideas into practical application. In the 1860s, Sedlmayr introduced a pilot system of refrigeration in his Munich brewery, and later expanded it. Dreher immediately recognized that his friend was on to something good, and designed an entirely new lager plant around refrigeration. In 1868 he purchased an existing brewery at Trieste and reconfigured it around his new refrigeration system. The choice of location was interesting, for according to *One Hundred Years of Brewing* the brewery in Trieste produced some of the worst beer in Europe. Many felt that good beer could not be made there. This did not turn out to be the case, and after Dreher's modifications the brewery at Trieste flourished as did his three other breweries.

The total operation became one of the largest commercial operations in Europe under single management. That Dreher was able to exercise effective control over these large operations, not to mention over the quality of beer being produced, is regarded by many as equal to his achievements in the scientific and technological areas.

Dreher's most lasting achievement, and the one most relevant to us as modern brewers, is his promotion and support of top-quality brewing ingredients. The use of such ingredients is crucial to achieving the full measure of Viennese character in both Vienna and Märzen/Oktoberfest beer styles. Moreover, this is an area where the Pilsen and Vienna brewing traditions converge.

A detailed survey of brewing materials will be given later, but a few comments are in order here. It is now known that barley variety is just as important to brewers as grape variety is to winemakers. The brewing analog of the noble *Vinifera* grapes (Cabernet Sauvignon, Chardonnay, etc.) is what is called today the family of Moravian barleys. The origin of this strain can be traced back centuries. While it mainly

came from the Moravian region of Bohemia, similar strains were cultivated in both Belgium and France. Strains of this barley have exceptional malting and brewing characteristics (to be discussed later) which set them apart from other two-row barleys. Malt from Moravian strains has in modern times been so closely identified with Pilsener beer, and in particular Pilsner Urquell, that it is typically called "Pilsener malt." This term will be retained in this book, though it is somewhat misleading since the cultivation of Moravian barley precedes Pilsner Urquell by several centuries.

As is typical of many ingredients that make up finer and elegantly-flavored foods, Moravian barley historically has been difficult to grow. It has a lower yield per acre than other varieties, and it tends to be more susceptible to adverse climatic and soil conditions. It is therefore to Dreher's credit that he insisted on these grains for malting, and no substitutes were permitted. While farmers generally regarded Moravian as a pain in the neck, they quickly learned that if they were to sell grain to Dreher, at that time the biggest game in town, it was going to be Moravian or nothing at all. Fortunately, "Pilsener malt" is available today to small-scale brewers and forms the backbone for the authentic recipes in Chapter 3.

The current situation with respect to colored malts is less favorable. This is in part because of the all-too-frequent modern practice of using lesser barley varieties for colored malts. It is rare to find a colored malt made from quality Moravian barley, and this situation presents many practical problems for those wishing to brew Viennese beers. Various strategies for dealing with these problems will be discussed later.

Dreher had exacting standards with respect to hop varieties as well. In particular, the Saaz hop from the Zatec region in Bohemia found favor with him and was widely used in his breweries. Dreher's beers were not as highly hopped as the pale beers from Pilsen. He was more like the Bavarians in this regard. Nevertheless, though there is a marked difference in hop flavor intensity in the two styles, Dreher's Vienna did share with Pilseners of his day certain unique aromatic characteristics derived from the Saaz hop.

Another hop variety that found favor with Dreher is the Styrian Golding hop, and in fact his family played an instrumental role in its cultivation. Although less well known today than the Saaz, it nevertheless is a nobly-flavored hop that does well in Vienna-style beers. The Styrian Golding variety was brought into England, and formed the backbone of the famous hop-growing area in and around Kent. A detailed analysis of these hops and possible alternatives will have to await later chapters. The larger point here is Dreher's exacting standards. Be it hop, grain or yeast, only the very best ingredients were acceptable to Dreher for his Vienna-style lagers.

Brewing of lager beer year-round began when refrigeration became a practical option. This led, among other things, to a standard Vienna style which generally had a slightly lower starting gravity and was aged over a shorter time than the festival version. Demand for this type of beer remained strong, and at the start of the 20th century Viennas, Pilseners and Münchners were the three major lager styles brewed on a regular basis. The first recipe in Chapter 3 is typical of the formulas brewed at the turn of the century.

In Bavaria, on the other hand, the traditional Märzen/Oktoberfest brewing process was retained. This was in part due to the popularity of the beer and the understandable reluctance on the part of Bavarian brewers to change a commercial success. Also important is the role of festivals in Bavaria (references 3 and 17), and in particular the October festivals. People expected a beer brewed in March for these festivals, and the term "Märzen" was generally used to designate a beer in this style. The Märzen/Oktoberfest recipe in Chapter 3 is typical of the formulations that were used for this beer style, which by the start of the 20th century was distinct from the standard Vienna style. In the post World War II era starting gravities dropped slightly, putting the Märzens into the standard Vienna range (reference 3), i.e. from 1.059 to 1.063 (14.5° to 15.5° P) to 1.050 to 1.055 (12.5° to 13.5° P). However, preference for the extended Märzen/Oktoberfest process remains strong today.

Märzens are currently being brewed in Bavaria using a shorter aging period, but these are the exception, not the rule.

THE FIRST DECLINE

Unfortunately and alas, the standard Vienna style did not fare very well in the early and middle part of the 20th century. In Europe it virtually disappeared. There are many reasons for this, but one was the enormous popularity of Pilsener-style beers. Brewers everywhere were strongly motivated to brew their own versions, and the Viennese were no exception to this.

A second factor was increasing popularity in the Austro-Hungarian territories of another pale colored beer, the export or Dortmunder-style lager. It would be a mistake to view export as a pale version of Vienna, for they have major differences that go well beyond color. Yet they do share a balanced malt and hop flavor which easily distinguishes them from hoppy Pilseners. Thus, brewers soon found it advantageous to brew Pilseners as their "bitter lager", with exports gradually replacing Viennas as the brewer's "mild lager." Here the term "mild" refers to hop flavor, for both exports and Viennas have traditionally been higher in alcohol content than Pilseners. This trend has continued to the present day. Indeed, if one were to identify two of Austria's most well-known beers today, they would likely be Steffl Pils and Gösser Special. The latter is a very fine export/Dortmunder-style beer, and the former is a highly-respected Pilsener. Both are pale without a trace of amber.

Probably the most important reason for the demise of the standard Vienna style was the use of inferior barley for malting colored grains. Dreher would never have permitted this, but after his death there was apparently no one around with his intellect and vision to prevent the practice in Austria. It is also very likely that the demise of the Austro-Hungarian empire during this period contributed to the style's decline.

THE NEW WORLD CONNECTION

Another major factor in the European demise of standard Vienna-style beers was the immigration of Vienna brewers to the Americas (both North and South). Such people included not only brewers from the city of Vienna, but from places throughout the old empire including outlying areas like Switzerland and the Alsace regions. This immigration occurred primarily in the very late 19th and early 20th centuries, decades after the waves of German immigrants that first came to the Americas. The reasons for this later immigration are complicated and diverse. The impending demise of the Austro-Hungarian empire was surely a factor. The changes in brewing conditions after Dreher's death were also a factor. That there were significant changes is clear from historical records. That not everyone agreed with what was going on and some simply got disgusted and left is therefore probable. While this is pure speculation, the fact that many of those who emigrated were brewers in the Dreher tradition—a striking example is given below—tends to reinforce this conjecture.

The bulk of this immigration was directed toward the Southwest, primarily Texas and Mexico, which for the purposes of this book can be regarded as one unit during this period. The reasons why this region was chosen are clear. The Midwest and East had at this time well-established brewing centers. The other major population centers at that time were the Southeast and Southwest. The former was not regarded as an option because of that region's strong tradition

States and Territories	1863	1875	1902	Increase in 1902 compared with 1863	Increase in 1902 compared with 1875
Alabama	—	401	68,500	68,500	68,099
Alaska	—	—	38,437	38,437	38,437
Arizona	—	527	24	24	503
Arkansas	—	95	11,122	11,122	11,027
California	81,412	302,287	840,140	758,728	537,853
Colorado	1,178	23,516	323,366	322,188	299,850
Connecticut	13,025	52,503	518,690	505,655	466,187
Dakotas	—	1,823	29,409	29,409	27,586
Delaware	712	5,646	105,392	104,680	99,746
Dist. of Columbia	3,580	21,573	228,647	225,067	207,074
Florida	—	—	10,305	10,305	10,305
Georgia	—	5,530	130,798	130,798	125,268
Hawaii	—	—	10,912	10,912	10,912
Idaho	—	915	18,091	18,091	17,176
Illinois	156,645	536,619	4,132,301	3,975,656	3,595,682
Indiana	53,843	181,053	995,003	941,160	813,950
Iowa	21,206	180,653	305,033	284,007	124,380
Kansas	4,138	23,592	8,759	4,621	14,833
Kentucky	52,111	114,070	534,750	482,639	420,680
Louisiana	—	30,910	245,202	245,202	214,292
Maine	2,207	11,527	—	2,207	11,527
Maryland	64,684	191,548	827,534	762,850	635,986
Massachusetts	112,000	479,597	1,831,829	1,719,829	1,352,232
Michigan	29,654	191,274	1,109,891	1,080,237	918,617
Minnesota	7,766	88,567	869,210	861,444	780,643
Mississippi	—	7	—	—	—
Missouri	138,631	397,033	2,996,910	2,858,279	2,599,877
Montana	—	3,967	191,947	191,947	187,980
Nebraska	868	22,867	259,549	258,681	236,682
Nevada	2,518	12,990	13,615	11,097	625
New Hampshire	25,945	139,482	335,787	309,842	196,305
New Jersey	183,830	485,600	2,463,178	2,279,348	1,977,578
New Mexico	321	1,190	5,575	5,254	4,385
New York	969,094	2,889,777	10,467,784	9,498,690	7,578,007
North Carolina	—	81	—	—	81
Ohio	240,781	480,114	3,489,050	3,248,269	3,008,936
Oklahoma	—	—	2,749	2,749	2,749
Oregon	1,547	7,257	174,423	172,786	167,166
Pennsylvania	348,862	964,364	5,567,100	5,218,238	4,602,466
Rhode Island	7,029	18,975	365,744	358,715	346,769
South Carolina	—	1,835	5,923	5,923	4,088
Tennessee	—	1,541	172,918	172,918	171,377
Texas	—	14,057	431,360	431,360	417,303
Utah	84	6,829	46,184	46,100	39,355
Vermont	1,371	1,195	—	1,371	1,195
Virginia	9,071	14,878	146,895	137,824	132,017
Washington	812	5,253	253,834	253,022	248,581
West Virginia	—	26,526	212,504	212,504	185,978
Wisconsin	62,048	440,614	3,675,566	3,613,518	3,234,952
Wyoming	—	2,792	6,892	6,892	4,100
Total bbls	2,506,803	8,383,720	44,478,832	41,882,029	36,095,112

Table 1: Summary of Sales of Malt Liquors by States, 1863–1902.

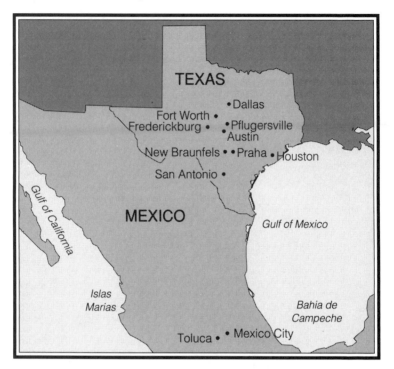

of alcohol prohibition, not to mention its legacy of slavery. Texas did have elements of this type of culture, but only on a narrow eastern rim of the state. The central and western parts were dramatically different.

Of the two, the central region was of greatest interest. It had one of the highest concentrations of central European immigrants in North America. Even today, traveling south through the Texas Hill Country towards Mexico one passes through towns like Fredericksburg, New Braunfels, and Pflugersville where in the 19th century, German was commonly spoken. There are also Bohemian towns like Praha, Texas where the older Czech language can still be heard. Most of these people immigrated in the middle of the 19th century. As in Wisconsin and elsewhere in the Midwest and East, they immediately started brewing. However, brewers in Texas and Mexico did not have the climatic advantage of the Great Lakes nor the ice they provided during winter months for proper beer storage during the summer. The inability to control temperature in conjunction with the vicissitudes of Tex/Mex summers proved to be fatal. The beer produced was reported to be of "exceptionally low quality." Not surprisingly, this period was marked by a series of brewery openings quickly followed by their closings (references 4 and 19). Interestingly, homebrewing became quite popular during this period. Virtually every community in the Hill Country had people engaged in this ancient art.

For the brewers who immigrated later, climate was not so much a problem, because refrigeration became available and dramatically altered the situation for brewing. Indeed, what emerged in the 1890s was truly a golden era. Table 1 (taken from reference 1) has representative statistics. For example, in 1879 a mere 14,000 barrels of beer were brewed in Texas, but by 1902 this increased to over 400,000 barrels. While this is small compared to the Eastern states, Texas was less populous then the East. Texas would be near the top of a chart showing barrels per person. Statistics for Mexico showed a similar pattern.

Given the cultural trends cited above, it is not surprising that the Southwest brewing industry was concentrated in a central strip that went south through the Hill Country to Mexico.

In the north, important breweries were located in Dallas. The Dallas Brewing Co. was founded in 1887, and the highly acclaimed Texas Brewing Co. in Forth Worth was founded in 1890. In the Southern part of the state, Houston had two important breweries. American Brewing was founded in 1893 and Houston Ice and Brewing Co. was founded in 1893. The most important brewing town in

Texas, however, was San Antonio, which is strategically located at the southern end of the Hill Country and benefitted from close cultural ties with Mexico. San Antonio had several breweries, but two deserve mention because they are still in operation. One is the San Antonio Brewing Co. (founded in 1883) which later became Pearl Brewing. The other is Lone Star Brewing (founded in 1884). Interestingly, none other than Adolphus Busch served as president of the company for a period. In fact, the Busch family was very active in Texas brewing prior to Prohibition, and the elegant and historic Adolphus Hotel in Dallas is named after Adolphus Busch.

The most important region of this period, however, was Mexico. The reason for this is that the most influential figure, quite literally the brains behind the show, was located there. He was a Mexican citizen named Santiago Graf. He actually immigrated earlier than most Viennese-oriented brewers, and started in 1875 with a top-fermentation brewery in Toluca, Mexico, a small community outside of Mexico City.

Graf was aware of the success of Dreher and Sedlmayr with bottom-fermenting lager yeast, yet he correctly realized he could not make lager beer given the Mexican climatic conditions. His ale was carefully brewed, and he used ice to avoid excessive temperatures. This product was very popular, and even brief surveys of brewing in the Americas invariably cite it as the first commercially viable beer brewed in the Southwest (for example page 10 in reference 20).

In 1882, Graf purchased an absorption ice machine from Germany. He then switched to the new lager yeast. The beer produced was an enormous success. *One Hundred Years of Brewing* states that it completely "...drove foreign beers out of the local market ...". In 1890 a new, modern lager brewery was constructed. It had a capacity of

Texas Brewing Co. Photo from the collection of the Texas/Dallas History and Archives Division, Dallas Public Library.

approximately 100,000 barrels, which was large for the time. This brewery served as a model not only for Texas and Mexico, but also for large parts of South America.

Santiago Graf, like Dreher and Sedlmayr, had uncompromising standards in regards to brewing ingredients. He found the wild six-row barley available in the Southwest to be totally unacceptable. While malt from Canadian barley had a good reputation with brewers in North America, he found it as well to be below his standards. Thus he imported all his grains from Europe. He did the same with his hops, for the varieties grown in North America (primarily in the state of New York) were too crudely flavored for his taste. Interestingly, the legacy of this orientation can be seen today. Most Central and South American breweries still tend to use far more European grains and hops than American.

Historical references indicate that the classic lager styles (Pilsener, Vienna and Munich) were widely brewed in the Americas during the latter part of the 19th and early 20th century. Also brewed was "American lager." This was defined during this period as any lager beer made with malt and adjuncts, the latter typically being unmalted cereals like corn and rice. "American lager," however, was not the dominant beer style, and indeed the practice of using "cheap inferior brewing materials" (i.e. adjuncts) was highly controversial during this period (reference 18).

It is interesting that regional differences in beer styles were starting to develop. For example, in the Northeastern United States the demand for ales was strong. The lagers produced tended to be highly hopped, having a Pilsener tilt. Smooth and rounded lagers roughly in the export and Munich styles generally found acceptance in the Midwest. For example, Anheuser-Busch regularly produced an all-malt dark beer called "Münchner", and a soft all-malt pale lager in addition to Budweiser, their "American lager".

Various types of beer were brewed in the Southwest, but it was the ambers which received the highest acclaim. Some references suggested that it was the alkaline character of the artesian well water found in San Antonio (and further south in Mexico) that was responsible for this (reference 21). However, it is the authors' view that the real factor was the strong influence Graf had over Southwestern brewing. He also pioneered the development of a major variation of the Vienna style, using a small amount of black malt in the formulation. This style will be discussed at length later. He did brew a variety of lighter-colored ambers, but apparently totally pale beers in the Pilsener style did not interest him to any great extent.

ALAMO BOTTLED BEER
"THE BEER AHEAD"
Everything the best-the very best that money can buy, coupled with modern facilities and the most skilled labor that accounts for the unapproachable quality of ALAMO BOTTLED BEER.
LONE STAR BREWING CO.
SAN ANTONIO, - - - - - TEXAS

The Lone Star Brewing Co. sells more than 65,000 barrels of beer annually and distributes throughout Texas, Mexico and California. Label courtesy of Mike Hennech.

Sadly and alas, these traditions were totally destroyed in Texas and the United States as a whole by Prohibition. After Repeal, the beers made had very little in common with those brewed in the golden era from 1900 to 1915. Adjuncts found an acceptance that would have been unthinkable in that earlier era. Old world styles, including Viennas, were dropped in favor of "American lager." This of course occurred throughout the country, and not only in Texas. There are many reasons why events took this turn, but one cannot overlook the role played by Prohibitionists and neo-Prohibitionists. This movement has always had a strong irrational element, and one aspect of this has been a definite prejudice against European culture, and in particular central European culture. The emotion surrounding World War I promoted this viewpoint even among those who should have known better. It is the authors' opinion that brewers overreacted to anti-European emotionalism by overly promoting themselves as "American brewers" producing "American beer," and thus neglecting traditional beer styles. Obviously, this issue is complicated and many other factors were involved.

Mexico had the good fortune not to have a Prohibition. However, something almost as bad for the brewing industry occurred, namely revolution. In the midst of the chaos no one with the intellect and vision of a Santiago Graf emerged to provide leadership. Cheaper brewing ingredients became acceptable, and the industry floundered during this period. Fortunately the changes were not as dramatic as in the United States, and there are still some Mexican beers being brewed today which can give some useful hints about the type of beer brewed earlier. This will be taken up in Chapter 5.

MODERN TIME—RESURRECTION

Happily, this chapter can be ended on a positive note, for Viennas are now back with us. Clearly, the emergence of serious homebrewing in the early 1970s is primarily responsible for their reintroduction. One cannot overstate the central role played by Fred Eckhardt's classic monograph on lager beers, *A Treatise on Lager Beer*, published in 1977 (reference 5). Of particular interest was the centerfold, showing lagers of various styles and colors. While these recipes are now somewhat dated, they were quite serviceable at the time. More to the point, they were capable of producing creditable beers which amply showed that lagers are far more than one-dimensional thirst quenchers. One can ask no more of a pioneering work like this. Today, it would be unthinkable to have a major competition without a category for "Vienna/Märzen/Oktoberfest." Moreover, there is invariably a respectable number of entries in this category. The quality of the entries is generally impressive in competitions the authors have judged.

The interest in Viennas among homebrewers spilled over in the 1980s to commercial brewing, particularly to microbreweries and brewpubs. The survey in Chapter 5 of commercial beers in the Vienna style contains a healthy fraction of brews from small operations.

In summary, it is safe to say that Viennese-style beers are back, alive and well, and in good loving hands. History has always been kind to this style in this regard! We can hope that this time they'll stay.

2

Qualitative Features of the Flavor Profile

OPINIONS—PAST AND PRESENT

The central issue to be resolved in this chapter is the following: what precisely are the major attributes that characterize authentic versions of the traditional Viennese beer style? To start, the authors thought it would be useful to give direct quotations from leading experts. They are given below.

The first quote is the author's translation of comments from a 1905 source (reference 2). Special note is made of the quality of the brewing ingredients used to make these beers, and similar comments can be found in other sources from this era. As noted earlier, the authors feel this point is of fundamental importance.

The second quote by a famous brewing consultant, reflects the era immediately before and after Prohibition (reference 6). The final version of Nugey's manual was not published until 1948, but this quote is from an earlier version published in the 1930s. It should be noted that Nugey's use of the English language is somewhat bizarre. Take for example the term "light golden." Fortunately, there is a number (i.e., 12 degrees Lovibond) to go with this description. Be assured that 12 degrees Lovibond (12° L) is a rather deep color. Indeed, Anchor Steam and Bass Ale are each around 10° L, to cite but two examples, and 12° L is a couple of degrees darker still. The authors have found that if one replaces the term "golden" everywhere in Nugey's manual with "amber" the discussions tend to make more sense. The same applies to the term "sweet." There are some styles of Vienna which finish with a slight sweetness. This, however, should be understated and much less evident than it is in a Munich helles, for example. In fact, the authors feel that Viennas come out best with a completely dry finish. Again, Nugey's comments seem to take on greater coherence with appropriate substitutions, in this case replacing "sweet" with "malty." Nugey's remarks about the balance of hop and malt flavors, on the other hand, are very well taken.

The big shocker is the quote by deClerck. He was not only a brewing scientist of accomplishment and depth, but also a practical hands-on brewer as well. Of special note was his measured and even-handed approach to brewing. Ad hoc opinions and dogmatic posturing were totally foreign to him. Thus, his comments convince us that the Viennas of his era were definitely of inferior quality. The authors came across this quote only a few years ago, and spent considerable time trying to get full meaning of the critique. Out of his search emerged four big points, hereafter called the "deClerck four." These are four points related to brewing procedures. They do not represent insurmountable problems as far as practical brewing is concerned, but are things to which we should be particularly sensitive when brewing beers in Vienna style. Chapter 4 is devoted in large part to the "deClerck four."

The final quotes are taken from Michael Jackson and

the AHA score sheets in current use. Both are accurate and useful, particularly the comments about strength. Strength is an attribute which often can be used to distinguish Viennas from other amber beers, better classified as milds.

- Assorted Opinions about Viennas -

Source/Time	Comment
Zimmerman (1905)	"...These beers have a good color with both malt fullness and hop bitter. They are brewed from only the best malt and hops..." (reference 2)
Nugey (1910–1919 and 1933–1940)	"...light golden color, not more than 12° L, neither malt nor hop flavors predominate, with sweet and bitter taste..." (reference 6)
deClerck (1935–1955)	"At one time a Vienna type of bottom fermenting beer was brewed. It had a color intermediate between that of Munich and Pilsener. The palate was at the same time aromatic and bitter, qualities which are not compatible, and it has almost disappeared from the market." (reference 7)
M. Jackson (1988)	Vienna—"Amber-red, or only medium dark, lager... Strengths vary." Märzen—"... has a malty aroma, and is a medium-strong version (classically, more than 5.5 percent

alcohol by volume) of the amber-red Vienna style. It is seasonal to the Oktoberfest." (reference 15).

American Homebrewers Association (1991)	"Amber to copper colored, usually brewed with a respectable alcohol content. Vienna style characteristically has a rich, toasted malt aroma and smooth malt flavor, counterbalanced with a clean bitterness of German hops. 5.0 to 6.0 percent alcohol by volume."

A COMPOSITE PROFILE

After reviewing the background material that was compiled for this monograph, the authors concluded that the following seemed to be the best descriptors for the traditional Vienna beer style:

1—Elegance
2—Softness
3—Complexity
4—Balance

There is one point that is common to all libations—be it beer, wine, or whatever. The elegance of the finished product is inevitably related to the quality of the ingredients used. For brewers the practical issue is whether the cost of the special malt and hops that are required to achieve this attribute is worth their use. For the Vienna style this issue seems clear. Vienna has always been an elegant city, and beer named after it should reflect this elegance.

Viennas aren't the only lagers with aspirations of

elegance. Certainly the classic Czech Pilseners (Pilsner Urquell and Budvar) can make such claims, as can the select but extraordinary Pilseners produced by some German breweries (e.g., Veltins and König Pils). There is a good reason for this: all use similar barley and hop varieties. What distinguishes Viennas is their color and soft finish. While Pilseners can be seen as concertos for hops, Viennas are balanced symphonies where all the ingredients gently make their points. It is here where brewing procedures are crucial. In fact, just about all of the issues associated with the "deClerck four" deal with procedure. Invariably, technical errors in brewing methods will lead to "astringent" and/or "hard" flavor tones which compromise the soft texture one seeks in Vienna beer.

Softness, however, should not come at the expense of complexity, otherwise the beer can degenerate into boring, one-dimensional blandness. Amber ales, most notably pale ales, gain complexity through fermentation products, cask conditioning and related matters. For Viennas complexity, if it is going to be there, must come from the malt and hops. Here the recipe used is crucial. As a general rule, several types of malt and several aromatic hop varieties are wanted, provided they are of high quality. This is quite different from pale ales, where a good quality malt and a top quality hop usually suffice. See for example the recipe in Terry Foster's monograph on pale ales (reference 8).

BREWING INGREDIENTS
AND GENERAL GUIDELINES

The following are general guidelines about brewing ingredients that have proven suitable for brewing standard Viennas, Märzen/Oktoberfests and variations of these styles. The section is meant to supplement the numerical data found in the next chapter.

   1. Color—The general guideline is 8° to 12°L. At the turn of the century, the beer which found most favor in the Dreher breweries had a color in the range 9° to 10° L. A similar style was brewed in the Southwest where it was usually called oscura or semi-oscura. A darker version in the range 10° to 12° L also was brewed in the Graf brewery and elsewhere. Noche Bueno at 12° L is a derivative of the type, and represents an upper limit to the amount of color that is appropriate to the style.

   Because of the importance of color to this style, an appendix has been included on the general subject of beer color. It contains practical procedures for measuring and predicting beer color. It is to be emphasized that brewing conditions strongly affect the color of the finished beer. Thus, some brewers might find that a particular recipe produces exactly the desired color, while others might find some adjustments are needed. The material in the appendix is designed for such situations.

   2. Gravity—The starting gravity (original extract, or OE) should be in the range 1.050 to 1.055 (12.5° to 13.5° P). The desired final gravity depends on the type of finish that is sought.   A dry finish is desirable, and this can be achieved with a final gravity (apparent extract, or AE) of 1.010 (2.5° P). A slightly longer mash at moderate conversion temperature, say 150 to 152 degrees F (66 to 67 degrees C), is needed for this.   Some excellent Viennas have been made with a slightly sweet finish, but in any case one should not have a final gravity above 1.014 (3.5° P). The strength of the resulting beer can be accurately approximated by the following modified Balling formula:

$$\text{Alcohol (by wt.)} = \frac{(.8192) \times (OE - AE)}{2.0665 - (.010665 \times OE)}$$

Typical values are as follows:

OE	AE	A (by wt.)	A (by vol.)
13.5° P (1.055)	2.5° P (1.010)	4.7%	5.9%
13.5° P (1.055)	3.5° P (1.014)	4.3%	5.3%
12.5° P (1.050)	2.5° P (1.010)	4.2%	5.3%
12.5° P (1.050)	3.5° P (1.014)	3.8%	4.7%

Any of these are acceptable for this style.

3. Base malt—In Dreher's time one malt was used, an amber-colored one produced from the same high quality Moravian barley used at Pilsen, but kilned (dried) at a higher temperature. In modern times malts of this color are available, but the quality of the barley used is highly variable, both in Europe and in North America. Thus, to achieve the best results it has been customary to start with a pale malt (which here is called the base malt), which can be had of high-quality. The base malt will constitute 75 percent of the grain bill and the remaining 25 percent will be colored malts as discussed below.

Moravian is the preferred barley for lager beer, as Chapter 1 indicated. This barley is to lager beer what Chardonnay grapes are to white wine. It is interesting that modern analysis of malt has made the reasons for this clear. Moravian barley has lower nitrogen (i.e., protein) levels than other two-row barley, and the spectrum of the proteins present is different. Moravian barley can be distinguished from other barley by an analysis of the proteins present in the grain (reference 9). Fortunately, quality Moravian barley is grown today not only in Bohemia, but also Belgium, France, Germany, and North America. Malt made from this barley, as noted earlier, is generally called Pilsener malt.

Perhaps the most widely available Pilsener malt for small scale brewers comes from German imports. It is

31

expensive, a characteristic of any authentic Pilsener malt, but is worth every penny. The authors have often been asked if the average small-scale brewer can use Central European malts, given the fact that they are "undermodified." Actually, the term "undermodified" is deceptive in this regard. Modification in malting refers to two separate things, protein modification and carbohydrate modification. The Pilsener malt from Germany will be slightly "undermodified" as far as carbohydrates are concerned, at least in comparison to English and North American malts. However, the protein is not undermodified. Indeed, because of their highly favorable protein structure, Moravian barley is quite easy to malt. The practical consequence of this characteristic is that a number of mashing systems can be used with these malts, including infusion mashes. One may wish to employ a decoction mash, but this system is not required. Pilsener malts, on the other hand, will provide enzymes that are capable of converting only the malt's own starch. Thus, they are not generally recommended for formulations calling for unmalted cereal grains like corn and rice.

Another genuine item is the strain grown in the United States called Moravian III. It does have a slightly higher nitrogen level and stronger enzyme system than the European Pilsener malts, but the differences are not major and in practical terms these barleys can be regarded as equivalent. The Moravian III strain is essentially under the control of the Coors Brewing Co., which typically will use the entire year's harvest. Thus, it is not a practical source for others. One can only wish that other maltsters in North America would contract to have more of this noble variety grown.

Second in desirability are standard two-row "lager malts." Examples are Klages and Harriton in North America and Triumph in Europe. If Pilsener malt is not available,

The Coors Microbrewery, a.k.a. Coors Pilot Brewery, is where Winterfest was brewed before it was distributed nationally.

then these can be used for the base malt. There will be, however, a definite decrease in both elegance and complexity of the malt characteristics of the finished beer. Brew two Viennas, one batch using Pilsener malt as the base malt and the other using Klages, and compare. There is no better way to make the point about the importance of barley variety!

Malt from six-row barley has not found favor in Vienna-style beers. In several trips to Bavaria, the authors questioned many brewmasters in both Munich and Kulmbach about this point, and the response was universal. They would absolutely not use a six-row malt in a proper Märzen/ Oktoberfest. This is not to say that six-row malt is inferior to two-row malt. Some sensational turn of the century "American lager" recipes are based on six-row malts and a small amount of cereal grains. In addition, the two best wheat beers the authors have tasted—German or American—have used six-row barley. But each beer style has its own requirements. To make the best possible beer in a given style, there is a definite appropriateness ranking of ingredients.

The biggest headache in preparing this book was to find a way to treat malt extracts, be they syrups or dried malt. They should not be used for either standard Viennas or for Märzen/Oktoberfest beers. This is not to say that extract-based beers are inferior to all-grain beers. There are many fine extract formulations out there. However, in a style like Vienna where the malt character is such a crucial issue, the extracts do not give the best results. The striking failure of amber lagers based on malt extracts that were introduced in the 1980s by various microbreweries illustrate this point.

The key to brewing a respectable amber lager with extract lies in the freshness of the extract. Various chemical changes start and continue once the concentrated wort is packaged—be it as a syrup or in dried form (reference 9, page

117). As with a cut apple, color change will occur via browning reactions, and flavors are affected as well. Some day technology may change this situation, for there is a strong interest in extracts among large commercial brewers. The best step in the short run would be to get extract producers to date their products.

4. Colored Malts—These will make up the final 25 percent of the grain bill, and therefore play a major role in both the color and complexity of the finished beer. Proper selection of these malts is therefore important.

The first point to be made relates to "Vienna malt". In the 19th century these were superior malts made from quality Moravian barley, but with a higher kilning temperature than was used for Pilsener malt. This process resulted in an amber-red grain, which, if used as the only malt, would typically give an amber colored beer of 8° to 10° L. Unfortunately, in the latter part of the 20th century it has become customary to use inferior barley to make malts called "Vienna."

The efforts to make Vienna malt from six-row barley have definitely not been successful. Dave Miller has commented on this point in his article on specialty malts (reference 23). There is a grainy harshness imparted that is totally out of character for a Viennese styled beer. He does point out, on the other hand, that these effects will moderate with extended cold storage.

What is truly disappointing is that Vienna malt from Europe, while generally made from two-row barley, is not that much better than Vienna malt made in the United States from six-row barley. Investigation into deClerck's critique of Vienna-style lagers revealed that indeed malt quality was a major issue. There is no one in the 20th century that understood malt as deeply as deClerck, both in practical and theoretical terms. Beer made from inferior grain like the 20th-century Viennas would be sure to get a negative response from him. Vienna style tends to bring out the worst qualities of inferior brewing ingredients.

The final confirmation of fears about "Vienna malt" came in a review article on European malt published in *Brewers Digest* (reference 11). This article contains interesting data including nitrogen (protein) levels of various malt types. There is a good deal more to malt quality than nitrogen level, but low levels generally mean top quality barley was used, while very high levels indicate inferior barleys were used. As expected, Pilsener malts had the lowest nitrogen levels followed by lager malts. The nitrogen levels of Vienna malt were orders of magnitude above both of these. While the author has not researched these issues concerning "Munich malt", there is a suspicion that the same comments above apply. What is truly outrageous is that the price of the currently available "Vienna malt" and "Munich malt" from Europe is the same as that of Pilsener malt. Given the quality of the barley variety used, the price of the colored malts should be reduced by at least a factor of four or five.

High quality colored malts can be obtained from Europe. Two examples from Germany are malts called "light crystal" and "dark crystal." They are produced by a unique malting process which consists of a relatively short time in a high-temperature kiln. This forms a hard crystal core in the kernel, which will be evident when the malt is milled. Only lager-quality barleys (like Triumph) are used, and they are a very welcome addition to the grain bill of any Viennese-style beer.

The strongest tradition of colored malts belongs to England, not surprising given their long history of amber and copper colored beers. Totally unlike the practice in the United States, only the best low-nitrogen barley varieties are generally used for colored malts, typically Archer, Arc-Royal, and Maris Otter. They make crystal malts (a malting process they invented) as well as standard caramel malts, and both are recommended. While it may seem crazy to recommend English malt for Viennese beer, quality is quality and the difference can be tasted.

It has recently come to our attention that a large and well-respected malting company on the West coast will soon market light and dark crystal malts. These are apparently produced under license in the U.K. In addition, Siebels of Chicago has announced it will start importing malt. A wide variety will be marketed (Pils, Best Pale Ale, and various color malts), and the accent will be on only top quality malts. This of course is very good news, for the "color malt problem" could simply disappear.

There is a version of the Vienna beer style which became quite popular in the Southwest where black or chocolate malts found favor. The amount used should be kept low, for only a fleeting hint of chocolate in both taste and smell is desirable. At too high a level, the beer color will exceed 12° L. Worse yet, the flavors would be altered in inappropriate ways. At low levels the complexity of the beer is enhanced in what is a nice, but secondary, flavor tone.

Some commercial brewers use syrups to convert their regular beers into dark beers. For example, the color in Michelob Classic Dark comes exclusively from such syrup additives, as it does in Shiner's Bock. The syrups do have the advantage of permitting almost total control over finished beer color, since they can be added at a late point in the brewing process. In the author's opinion, however, this control comes at too high a price. Their flavoring is not beer-like, and has caramel candy tones which are not welcome in the Vienna style.

5. Hops—As in other continental lager formulations,

aroma hops are recommended, and of these none match the Saaz in desirability. Saaz hops contribute a gently fruity flavor, taste and smell that can only be described as elegant. This character is mainly due to the unique oil content of this hop (reference 9). Traditionally, Saaz has been valued in lager brewing, for it can be used at very high concentrations without a lingering hop bitterness in the beer's aftertaste. Saaz hops, like other aroma hops, are unstable in storage. There will always be a discernable drop in alpha acids requiring recipe reformulation. In addition, slight putrid tones will be detectable in the hops during storage. These usually are removed in the kettle boil, however.

Consideration should be given to using other aroma hop varieties as well, for a number of high quality varieties are available. The diversity can add to the complexity of the finished beer. The Styrian Golding hop was certainly used in Dreher's time as noted in Chapter 1, and it makes an excellent bittering hop with, for example, Saaz hops used for middle addition and aroma.

German hops are also welcome additions to the kettle. Tettnanger, with its gentle and elegant spiciness, is highly recommended. The same is true of Hallertauer and its derivatives. The newer German varieties, most notably Perle, can be used in a pinch. However, their flavors are cruder than Tettnanger or Hallertauer.

American hops may be used with caution. Certainly, the European aroma hop varieties grown in the Northwest like Tettnanger are recommendable. This is also true of Hallertauer, which will emerge in the future under various disguises like Mt. Hood. Fuggles or Willamette will do in a pinch, but other varieties are unacceptable. Cascade hops, which make such remarkably favorable contributions to pale ales, are a disaster in Viennas. Lager brewers generally find their floral aroma and taste to be undesirable. The same

Brewkettle at the Pittsburgh Brewing Co.

can be said of modern high-alpha-acid hops like Nugget, Chinnok, etc. Cheap American hops like Cluster should be avoided at all costs.

The bitterness units (IBU) of the recipes in the next chapter will generally be in the mid-20s. It is to be emphasized, however, that this can be a misleading number. What is desired is a perfect flavor balance between malt and hops. Different brewing systems will extract different percentages of hop flavoring constituents (bitterness or iso-alpha-acids is but one component). Thus, the brewer should be prepared to modify the recipes to achieve balance. A single number cannot capture all of the important effects here, and one's palate is the best guide.

The dispute about pellets versus whole hops is a large one. There is not sufficient room in this monograph to do justice to both sides of this argument, though one of the authors attempted to do this in his book on brewing science (reference 9). It is the authors' opinion that preference should be given to whole hops when they are fresh. The pelletization process is rough on hops, particularly on their aromatic constituents. This is the primary reason pellets do less well than fresh whole hops. On the other hand, the noble low alpha-acid hops recommended for Viennas, notably the Saaz, store much better as pellets and as a consequence can be preferred over old whole hops in some circumstances. Highly compressed hops offer a middle ground that is worthy of consideration. Moreover, both Saaz and Styrian Golding are available in this form. In the future new CO_2 hop extracts will probably change the entire picture.

6. Water—A wide variety of water supplies can be used to brew Vienna-style beers. The only thing to avoid is water with a high sulfate content. Amber ales and amber lagers differ in regard to water composition. As Terry Foster

(reference 8) points out, it is the unique reactions between sulfate ions and the Kent hops which so attractively adds to the complexity of English pale ales. In Viennas the effect of these reactions is different, producing harsh and unpleasant notes. As a general rule, one should not use water whose sulfate content (i.e., concentration of SO_3 ions) exceeds 50 milligrams per liter. Below 25 milligrams per liter is an even better standard.

Some carbonate hardness in the mash water, on the other hand, is welcome. The dark malts bring sufficient acidity so that establishing a mash pH in the desired range (5.2 to 5.4) is usually not a problem, even if the alkalinity goes up to 300 milligram per liter. The carbonates, by neutralizing the acids in the dark malts, add to the softness of the finished beer.

The authors have found that alkaline water is less efficient in the sparge. The carbonates have a tendency to extract undesirables. Alkalinity in water can be removed by boiling and aeration. The use of distilled water is also a viable option for the sparge. In either case, a small amount of calcium chloride ($CaCl_2$) usually helps in restraining an undesirable increase in pH during the sparge. Gypsum (calcium sulfate) should be avoided. The same is true of so-called Burton salts, which are a mixture of gypsum and magnesium sulfate plus sodium chloride.

7. Yeast—there is a paradox here that will not be resolved in this monograph. There is ample evidence that the traditional Vienna had a pronounced aromatic, fruity, winey flavor tone. Vienna has always been a wine center as well as a major brewing area, and it has been reported that such flavor elements found favor there. deClerck's critique, on the other hand, suggests that this characteristic may well be responsible for the style's demise in Europe. There is absolutely no doubt that this flavor tone comes from

selected yeast strains. Some produce it, while others do not. Thus, brewers of Vienna beer are confronted with an issue similar to that of brewers of wheat beers. Do you use an "authentic yeast strain" with that all-too-special flavor, or use a "clean and neutral strain"? Modern brewers have tended to opt for the latter. For example, when the Anchor Brewery decided to make a wheat beer, they chose to use their own ale yeast, definitely a "clean strain," as opposed to a phenol-producing wheat beer yeast. There is some evidence that suggests that Santiago Graf made a similar choice for his Vienna beers.

A variety of neutral lager yeasts are available and can be used to brew Vienna beers. The authors' favorites are the Weihenstephen yeast strains, for they tend to promote rounded, malty flavors. The popular W-34/70 is an obvious choice. Actually, W-308 (sometimes known as "Weisenheimer") (reference 12) does very well with Viennas. Also recommended are the Wyeast liquid cultures. Wyeast No. 2308 is the same as W-308. The so-called Bavarian lager yeast (Wyeast No. 2206) behaves like a Weihenstephan strain and is highly recommended.

The authors have had practical experience with only one "authentic strain." This came from the American Type Culture Collection in Rockville, Md. It is ATCC 2704 and described as "type Saaz pitching yeast." The authors have dubbed it "tutti-fruity," for it indeed is a ferocious ester producer. Ester production can be restrained to some extent by massive oxygenation of the chilled wort before pitching, but even then the fruitiness of the finished beer can be overpowering. Blending is perhaps the best approach if a strain like this is used. This practice has done well in Pilsen, where one of many yeast strains used is a "tutti-fruity" lookalike. Even a one-to-one blend of a batch fermented with ATCC 2704 with a batch brewed with a neutral strain greatly helps. A three-to-one blend gives a finished beer with a gently fruity tone. This enhances complexity, and beers like this are likely to do well in competitions. They, however, may not be the best drinking beers because the fruitiness becomes tiring.

MÄRZEN/OKTOBERFEST

Traditionally, the festival beers have been scaled-up versions of standard Viennas, or more accurately the latter are scaled down versions of the former. Starting gravities for the Oktoberfest/Märzen style were typically in the range 1.059 to 1.065 (14.5° to 16° P). Once the extra strength is taken into account, the festival beers should be similar in attributes to the Viennas.

The article by Narziss (reference 3) gives an overall account of current brewing practice for festival beers. There has been a definite drop in the starting gravity. For examples Narziss reports data on nine beers. The lowest starting gravity was 1.051 (12.5° P), and the highest was 1.055 (13.5° P). Thus, today's festival beer is very close to yesterday's standard Vienna.

The color data is quoted in degrees EBC (°EBC). These units cannot be accurately translated into degrees Lovibond. However, they ranged roughly from light amber (7° to 8° L) to dark amber (11° to 13° L).

There was also a great diversity in the beer's finish. This varied from "soft and malty" with a "mild bitter" to "malty/aromatic" with a "strong bitter." Apparently, modern brewers of these beers simply do their own thing, as opposed to being a slave to particular stylistic considerations. After all, these beers are brewed with festival time in mind!

The recipe given in the next chapter is based on the traditional formulation, primarily to document such brewing practice. The reader should be advised that it is a much bigger beer that one is likely to find at the typical European Oktoberfest celebration. No doubt there is a definite consumer preference for the lower gravity versions, and with a starting gravity in the range 1.051 to 1.055 (12.5° to 13.5° P), they can hardly be called weak beers.

3

The Recipes

This chapter contains recipes that reflect the broad family of Viennese-style beers. A variety of brewing systems and procedures can be used for each recipe, and brewers should not shy away from using their own. The specific procedure used by the authors is given below.

The total amount of water used for the mash and sparge was 4/3 the brew size. Thus the one-barrel batch used a total of

$$4/3 = 1\ 1/3 \text{ barrels}$$

The small five gallon batch used a total of

$$(4/3) \times 5 = 6\ 2/3 \text{ gallons}$$

An equal amount of water was used for the mash and sparge. Thus, for the barrel batch the water used in both the mash and for sparging was

$$\frac{1\ 1/3}{2} = 2/3 \text{ barrels}$$

while

$$\frac{6\ 2/3}{2} = 3\ 1/3 \text{ gallons}$$

was used for the five gallon batch.

The temperature profile used in the mash was the following:

strike in	139° to 140° F (59° to 60° C)
	30 minutes
sugar conversion	154° F (68° C) 45 minutes
strike out	160° F (71° C)

The temperature of the sparge water was 170° F (77° C).

The starting gravity should be in the midpoint of the range cited if a 70 percent yield is achieved. For example, in the standard Vienna there is a gravity range of 12.5 to 13.5° P. The midpoint, 13° P, is equivalent to 35.44 lbs. of extract per barrel, which with a 70 percent yield gives

$$\frac{35.44}{.7} = 50.6 \text{ pounds}$$

of malt in a barrel (31 gallons), or what is the same,

$$\frac{50.6}{31} = 1.63 \text{ pounds of malt per gallon}$$

In actual brews, yields will vary from 60 percent to 75 percent so adjustments in the grain bill may be needed.

Generally, there will be an approximate 85 percent recovery of liquid in the sparge. This means

$$(1\ 1/3) \times .85 = 1.33 \times .85 = 1.13 \text{ barrel}$$

of wort will be transferred to the kettle in the barrel batch, while

$$(6\ 2/3) \times .85 = 6.67 \times .85 = 5.67 \text{ gallons}$$

will be recovered in the smaller batch. With 10 percent evaporation in the boil this will bring the volume down to the size designated in the recipe for fermentation.

Hop usage requires more detailed discussion, for it is the area in which brewers are likely to make the most adjustments in the recipes. The standard unit of

$$mg/L = \text{milligrams/liter}$$
$$= 10^{-3} \text{ grams / liter} = \text{parts per million}$$

is used. The reader should note that figures for hops as quoted in iso-alpha-acids in mg/L is not exactly the same as IBU, "International Bitterness Units." The latter is an empirical quantity, and the procedures used also take into account hop constituents other than iso-alpha-acids. Thus an iso-alpha-acid level of 25 mg/l in chilled wort might be measured at an IBU of 26 to 27. However, losses during processing would reduce both into the low to middle 20s, and the differences are not of great significance.

The hop quantities cited in the recipes have assumed a 4 percent alpha-acid hop and a 20 percent kettle utilization rate (KUR) for whole hops, and 25 percent for pellets. These rates seem to be typical of what most systems will yield with a 30 minute contact time of hop and boiling wort.

Suppose, to cite some examples, that an iso-alpha-acid concentration of 25 mg/L was sought in the chilled wort as in the standard Vienna recipe. First, suppose pellets of 4 percent alpha-acid are used. It now is generally accepted that multiple additions of pellets to the kettle do not achieve much (pelletization is indeed rough on certain hop constituents!). So we assume they are added at one fixed time before strike out to achieve a definite KUR. Let us say the KUR is 25 percent (typical for a 30 minute boil time). Then

$$25 / .25 = 100 \text{ mg/L}$$

of alpha-acids will be needed. A 4 percent alpha-acid-hop requires

$$100 / .04 = 2500 \text{ mg/L} = 2.5 \text{ g/l}$$

of hops. This translates into

$$2.5 \times .134 \times 5 = 1.675$$

ounces per 5 gallons (g/l = .134 oz/gal), or

$$2.5 \times .26 = .65$$

pounds per barrel (g/l = .26 lbs/bbl)

    If whole hops are used, then multiple hop additions are desirable. In this case the above analysis has to be applied to each addition, and then the parts summed up to give a whole. To illustrate this calculation the authors' favorite blend will be used. This consists of: First, Tettnanger hops at 4 percent alpha-acid which are boiled for 45 minutes at a KUR of 25 percent; second, add Styrian Goldings at 5 percent alpha-acid which are boiled for 30 minutes at a KUR of 20 percent; finally Saaz whole hops at 3 percent which are boiled 15 minutes at a KUR of 10 percent. The final data needed to complete this example is the fraction of iso-alpha-acids each addition contributes to the final 25 mg/L of iso-alpha-acids. Suppose we require the first contribute 35 percent of the bitterness, the second 50 percent, and the third 15 percent. The analysis for this ensemble is summarized in the following:

total iso-alpha-acid = 25 mg/L

First Hop—Tettnanger (4 percent)
- desired iso-alpha-acid (fraction) = .35 (35 percent)
- iso-alpha-acids required = 25 × .35 = 8.75 mg/L
- KUR fraction = .25 (25 percent)
- alpha-acid required = 8.75/.25 = 35 mg/L
- hop-alpha-acid fraction = .04 (4 percent)
- hop addition = 35/.04 = 875 mg/L = .875 g/l

Second Hop—Styrian Goldings (5 percent)
- desired iso-alpha-acid (fraction = .5 (50 percent)
- iso-alpha-acids required = 25 × .5 = 12.5
- KUR fraction = .2 (20 percent)
- alpha-acid required = 12.5/.2 = 62.5 mg/L
- hop alpha-acid fraction = .05 (5 percent)
- hop addition = 62.5/.05 = 1250 mg/L = 1.25 g/l

Third Hop—Saaz (3 percent)
- desired iso-alpha-acid (fraction) = .15 (15 percent)
- iso-alpha-acid required = .15 × 25 = 3.75
- KUR fraction = .10 (10 percent)
- alpha-acid required = 37.5 mg/L
- hop alpha-acid fraction = .03 (3 percent)
- hop addition = 37.5/.03 = 1250 mg/L = 1.25 g/l

Thus, one adds 1.25 grams per liter of Saaz, the late hop, 1.25 grams per liter of Styrian, the middle hop, and .875 grams per liter of Tettnanger. In a barrel batch this amounts to

$$1.25 \times .26 = .325 \text{ lbs/bbl}$$

for each of the later two hop additions, and

$$.875 \times .26 = .2275 \text{ lbs/bbl}$$

for the first. The reasons for the detailed calculations is that the bitterness extracted will vary dramatically (as the numbers above indicate) with hop variety (alpha-acid), hop type (whole or pellet), and the way they are used (amount and KUR). The figures quoted in the recipes are meant to get brewers in the right ballpark. The calculations cited will refine this, but in the end it is the brewers palate that will dictate.

The **Basic Dreher Vienna** is the standard Vienna formulated in the traditional style. As noted earlier many modern Märzen/Oktoberfest beers are formulated in exactly this way. So do not be surprised if this "standard Vienna" comes out like a "festbier" you may have tasted!

One sees some variations on the basic recipe which include a "Bavarian touch." This amounts to keeping the grain bill as cited but raising the mashing temperatures to achieve a higher residual extract (OE = 1.013 to 1.016, 3.5° to 4° P). Then reduce the hop level by approximately 20 to 25 percent. A definite sweetness will result, and it should be kept under control to avoid highly unattractive, cloying flavor tones.

The next recipe is the southwestern beer, versions of which are still brewed in Mexico, which dates back to Santiago Graf's period. For this reason it is called the **Graf Version of the Standard Vienna**. It is characterized by the

Several million litres are drunk from massive mugs in the breweries' beer tents put up on the Theresien meadow for every Oktoberfest in Munich. Photo courtesy of the German National Tourist Office.

use of a very small amount of black malt which deepens its color to the dark point of the acceptable color range for Viennas. The black malt is cracked and added after 45 minutes in the rest at 154 degrees F (68 degrees C). This rest is extended an additional 15 minutes (for a total of 1 hour) before striking out at 160 degrees F (71 degrees C).

Both starting gravities and hop rates have been dropped world wide. A modern version of the standard Vienna which reflect these trends has therefore been included. The recipe is called *Modern Vienna Mild*, and commercial examples are cited in the final chapter. Extract brewers should note that among the general family of beers in the Vienna style, this one has done the best in competitions among the various extract-based recipes quoted in this chapter. As noted earlier the freshness of the extract used is a highly relevant issue, as is the quality of the grains constituting the colored malts. The hop rate of the prize winning extract formulations the authors surveyed tended to be slightly higher (5 to 10 percent) than that quoted in the *Modern Vienna* recipe. Thus, extract brewers may wish to make analogous adjustments to this recipe.

The final two recipes are "festbiers," the first being the *Traditional Märzen/Oktoberfest Formulation.* Historical references (most notably reference 18) were compatible with the recipes the authors obtained from their visits to Germany. Thus, there is a great deal of confidence regarding its authenticity. As noted earlier, most Bavarian brewers now use a version of the *Standard Vienna* recipe for their "festbier." There are, nevertheless, a few small Bavarian brewers who produce the traditional version, and they are very much worth seeking out. It is indeed a sensational formulation.

The final "festbier" is a highly unorthodox formulation that was brewed in the Austro-Hungarian Empire around the turn of the century. The grain bill contains both malted barley and a small amount of malted wheat. As a consequence of including wheat, formulations like this likely drew scorn from Dreher and his fellow brewers. Indeed, there is evidence which suggests that beers like this one were "country beers," i.e., beers brewed in rural areas outside of Vienna for farmers and others in these areas. Thus it has been named *Viennese Country Beer.* In modern times, it is not necessary to belittle beers with such a humble origin—after all, lambics have a similar heritage!

Those interested in brewing beers for competitions can

forget this one however, and it is the only recipe in this chapter which was not refined by results from competitions. Its wheat character is too subdued to qualify for a weizenbier. On the other hand, the fact that some malted wheat is used in the formulation will be evident both in the beer's flavor, and in its body and viscosity. This character will lead to low scores if it is entered as a Vienna. What we have here is therefore "homebrew" in the traditional sense of this word, i.e. a formulation which defies categorization.

The slightly higher hop change in the last two formulations was included to account for the reduction in kettle utilization in these higher gravity festival beers (reference 9).

BASIC DREHER VIENNA

Batch Size	5 Gallons (Grain)	5 Gallons (Extract)	1 Barrel (Grain)
Grain Bill			
Pale malt (two-row, Pilsener quality):	7.5 lb (3.38 kg)	——	45 lb (20.25 kg)
German light crystal malt:	6 oz (170 g)	6 oz (170 g)	2.25 lb (1.01 kg)
German dark crystal malt:	6 oz (170 g)	6 oz (170 g)	2.25 lb (1.01 kg)
English caramel malt (120° L):	6 oz (170 g)	6 oz (170 g)	2.25 lb (1.01 kg)
Pale malt syrup:	——	4 lb (1.8 kg)	——
Light dry malt extract:	——	3 lb (1.35 kg)	——

Hops
4 percent alpha-acid equivalent blend of aroma hops (see text)

	1.7 oz (48 g)	1.7 oz (48 g)	10 oz (284 g)

Data

Water:	See Chapter 2
Original Gravity:	1.050–1.055 (12.5°–13.5° P)
Terminal Gravity:	1.010–1.014 (2.5°–3.5° P)
Approximate IBU:	25
Approximate Color:	8°–10° L
Yeast:	see Chapter 2

GRAF VERSION OF THE STANDARD VIENNA

Batch Size	5 gallons (grain)	5 gallons (extract)	1 barrel (grain)
Grain Bill			
Pale Malt (two-row, Pilsener quality):	7.75 lb (3.5 kg)	—	48 lb (22 kg)
German light crystal malt:	4 oz (113 g)	4 oz (113 g)	1.5 lb (6.75 kg)
German dark crystal malt:	4 oz (113 g)	4 oz (113 g)	1.5 lb (6.75 kg)
English caramel malt (120° L):	4 oz (113 g)	4 oz (113 g)	1.5 lb (6.75 kg)
Black malt (two-row):	3 oz (85.1 g)	3 oz (85.1 g)	1 lb (.045 kg)
Pale malt syrup	—	4 lb (1.8 kg)	—
Light dry malt extract:	—	3 lb (1.35 kg)	—

Hops

4 percent alpha-acid equivalent blend of aroma hops (see text)

1.7 oz (48 g)	1.7 oz (48 g)	10 oz (284 g)

Data

Water:	see Chapter 2
Original Gravity:	1.050–1.055 (12.5°–13.5° P)
Terminal Gravity:	1.010–1.014 (2.5°–3.5° P)
Approximate IBU:	25
Approximate Color:	10°–12° L
Yeast:	see Chapter 2

MODERN VIENNESE MILD

Batch Size	5 gallons (grain)	5 gallons (extract)	1 barrel (grain)
Grain Bill			
Pale malt			
(Pilsener quality):	6.75 lb (3.04 kg)	——	42 lb (1.89 kg)
German light			
crystal malt:	4 oz (113 g)	4 oz (113 g)	1.5 lb (0.675 kg)
German dark			
crystal malt:	4 oz (113 g)	4 oz (113 g)	1.5 lb (0.675 kg)
English caramel			
malt (20° L):	4 oz (113.4 g)	4 oz (113.4 g)	1.5 lb (0.675 kg)
Pale malt syrup	——	4 lb (1.8 kg)	——
Pale dry malt			
extract:	——	2 lb (0.9 kg)	——

Hops
4 percent alpha-acid equivalent blend of aroma hops (see text)

	1.3 oz (35 g)	1.3 oz (35 g)	7.8 oz (222 g)

Data

Water:	see Chapter 2
Original Gravity:	1.044–1.046 (11°–11.5° P)
Terminal Gravity:	1.010–1.012 (2.5°–3° P)
Approximate IBU:	18–20
Approximate Color:	5°–7° L
Yeast:	see Chapter 2

TRADITIONAL OKTOBERFEST/MÄRZEN

Batch Size	5 Gallons (grain)	5 Gallons (extract)	1 Barrel (grain)
Grain Bill			
Pale malt (two-row Pilsener quality):	8.5 lb (3.38 kg)	——	53 lb (23.85 kg)
German light crystal malt:	6 oz (170 g)	6 oz (170 g)	2.25 lb (1.01 kg)
German dark crystal malt:	6 oz (170 g)	6 oz (170 g)	2.25 lb (1.01 kg)
English caramel malt (20° L):	6 oz (170 g)	6 oz (170 g)	2.25 lb (1.01 kg)
Pale malt syrup	——	4 lb (1.8 kg)	——
Light dry malt extract:	——	4 lb (1.8 kg)	——

Hops

4 percent alpha-acid equivalent blend of aroma hops (see text)

	1.8 oz (50 g)	1.8 oz(50 g)	12 oz (340 g)

Data

Water:	see Chapter 2
Original Gravity:	1.059–1.063 (14.5°–15.5° P)
Terminal Gravity:	1.012–1.016 (3°–4° P)
Approximate IBU:	25
Approximate Color:	9°–11° L
Yeast:	see Chapter 2

VIENNESE COUNTRY BEER

Batch Size	5 gallons (grain)	5 gallons (extract)	1 barrel (grain)
Grain Bill			
Pale malt	6 lb (2.7 kg)	—	37 lb (16.65 kg)
Wheat malt	2.5 lb (1.13 kg)	2.5 lb (1.13 kg)	15.5 lb (6.98 kg)
German light crystal malt:	9 oz (255 g)	9 oz (255 g)	3.5 lb (1.58 kg)
German dark crystal malt:	9 oz (255 g)	9 oz (255 g)	3.5 lb (1.58 kg)
Light malt syrup	—	4 lb (1.8 kg)	—
Light dry malt extract:	—	1.25 lb (.56 kg)	—

Hops

4 percent alpha-acid equivalent blend of aroma hops

1.8 oz (50 g)	1.8 oz (50 g)	12 oz (340 g)

Data

Water:	see Chapter 2
Original Gravity:	1.059–1.063 (14.5°–15.5° P)
Terminal Gravity:	1.014–1.016 (3.5°–4° P)
Approximate IBU:	25
Approximate Color:	9°–11° L
Yeast:	see Chapter 2

4

Practical Tips
on Brewing Vienna Beer

Amber lagers are no more difficult to brew than other lager styles. A further advantage is that even if one fails to achieve the attributes of the traditional Vienna style, the result will usually be a good drinking beer anyway. There are, nevertheless, a few points that merit attention, and the purpose of this chapter is to cite these. As noted earlier, deClerck's sharp critique of the Viennese beers of his day is particularly relevant.

WORT PRODUCTION

The most important item of the "deClerck four" is related to wort production. In particular, it is essential that one avoid rough treatment of wort while it is still hot. For example, excessive stirring of the mash and/or turbulent wort transfer can have deleterious effects on the flavor stability of the finished beer. One of the authors discussed this point at length in *Principles of Brewing Science* (reference 9). Essentially what happens is that certain malt-based materials get oxidized and are passed on to the packaged beer, where they then play the role of oxidizing agents.

These effects are important for any beer, but for Viennas they are doubly important. First, the amber malts are rich in the offending materials. Secondly, the astringent bitterness that develops in the packaged beer (or perhaps even earlier) stands out like a sore thumb in an otherwise soft Vienna finish. deClerck's criticism of Viennese beers resulted not only from low malt quality, but also from the rather sloppy wort production procedures used. Interestingly, there is also another side to this story. With carefully prepared wort, the malt materials will be passed on to the finished beer in their reduced form. In this case, they will act as flavor protectors as opposed to oxidizers. This is why some amber and dark beers can have such a striking flavor stability.

The authors have used both infusion and decoction mashes with the recipes given in this book, and found there was very little difference in results from the two procedures. A decoction mash did tend to give slightly better yields and a slightly deeper malt flavor. On the other hand, there is also much more handling of hot wort in a decoction mash, and hence the oxidation issues discussed above tend to be more problematic.

The favorable protein structure of Pilsener malt makes a low temperature rest in the mash unnecessary. In commercial practice it is not uncommon to mash-in at 138 to 140 degrees F (58 to 60 degrees C). The purpose of the rest is to degrade various "gums" in the malt. This rest is not essential, but it generally will lead to a better run-off during the sparge. Conversion temperatures range from 150 to 156 degrees F (66 to 69 degrees C). The lower temperature gives an attenuated mash, which the author prefers for this type of beer. Typically, a 45 minute rest is appropriate. Half of this time is generally needed at the higher temperature. The authors have also found that it is not necessary to greatly increase the temperature for sparging. Leaving the mash at the conversion temperature, (or slightly higher) and sparging with water at 166 to 168 degrees F (74 to 76 degrees C) is satisfactory. The main advantage of not heating the mash is avoiding the possible caramelization of grains that can occur in attempting to bring the mash into the 166 to 168 degrees F (74 to 76 degrees C) temperature range.

FERMENTATION AND AGING

Once the questions relating to yeast strains discussed earlier have been resolved, then the fermentation of Viennas is the same as for any lager. Each yeast strain has a preferred environment, and that is the one that should be used. For example, German yeasts do well in the cold range, say 48 to 55 degrees F (8 to 13 degrees C). If a healthy yeast crop is pitched, then generally eight to 12 days will be needed. The fermentation should be allowed to go to completion in a single vessel to insure that all the undesirable by-products like diacetyl have been properly reduced. The Märzen/Oktoberfest process is an exception, and is discussed below. A 24 to 72 hour cooling period at 34 to 38 degrees F (1 to 3 degrees C) is also desirable before transfer.

There is considerable diversity of opinion among modern brewing experts regarding the proper time to age lager beer. One sometimes gets the impression that given any particular aging period, there is an expert out there advocating it as the optimal period of cold storage. Rather than add to this conflicting advocacy, the authors decided simply to relate what was their general experience with the test brews prepared for this book. These beers were aged in Cornelius kegs, which were stored in a refrigerator at 34 to 36 degrees F (1 to 2 degrees C). The kegs had the usual gas and liquid lines, and in addition a third sampling line whose tube extended 1/3 of the way into the tank. This permitted sampling during aging in such a way that the yeast sediment was not disturbed, and the aging beer was not compromised in any other way.

On the basis of these test brews, the following was a normal pattern for the type of malt and yeast recommended in Chapter 3. After a brief period of aging (say 24 to 36 hours), the beer is brilliantly clear. This is one of the side benefits of using top quality Pilsener malts with their favorable protein structure. Yeasty/sulfury tones will be evident at this point along with intense "smoky/malty" flavors. The latter is a characteristic fundamental to many Pilsener malts, and it will be evident in any young beer whose grain bill has a high fraction of this malt type.

There is a rapid decrease in these green beer characteristics over the next two weeks. In fact, a stable and acceptable beer can be had at this point if filtration is used. A 1-micron filter (or smaller) is needed, which has its own disadvantages (see below). Many commercial breweries which have a shortage of storage tanks elect to package their lager beer after a two week aging period (three weeks total). Longer aging is better for Viennas.

After the fourth week of cold storage, the green beer characteristics will have diminished to a point where they are scarcely discernable. The smoky/malty tones will have rounded out to an elegant malty character, typical of high quality malt types. Now only a gentle polish filtration (around 3 micron) is required.

If filtration is not used, then further improvement and reduction of green beer characteristics can be obtained by an additional 3 to 4 weeks of aging. There is very little benefit in going beyond a total of 7 to 8 weeks of aging, unless of course one elects to go all the way with the classic 6 to 8 month "March/October" option. This extended aging period requires special mention, for it is very much a viable option for brewers of amber lagers. The fact that Bavarian brewers, who currently are at the forefront of high technology brewing, still hold this process in high regard is a formidable point. Nevertheless, certain key requirements need to be satisfied if best results are to be achieved.

First, very low temperatures are needed. The general rule is a maximum of 35 degrees F (2 degrees C), and preferably storage is at 32 degrees F (0 degrees C). At higher temperatures, say 41 degrees F (5 degrees C), beer flavors will start to deteriorate after a time.

Second, the beer should be transferred to storage before the primary fermentation is complete. This is typically done when the gravity falls into the 1.016 to 1.018 (4° to 4.5° P) range. Thus, a closed stainless steel vessel will be needed. It should also be pointed out that to produce bottled beer with this process, a counterpressure fill system is required (see below). On the other hand, the process is a natural for a draft set-up where beer is dispensed from the storage tank. There is one major drawback of the draft option, which is of great practical significance. Namely, beer brewed in March may be consumed before October arrives!

The final point to be made about the Märzen/Oktoberfest process is that extended aging works only if the pitching yeast is in proper condition with respect to bacterial counts and mutation. Tests to check this are discussed below. One cannot underestimate the practical value of these procedures.

FILTRATION

The authors have been using a Zahm and Nagel filtration unit for over 10 years, and strongly recommend it or an equivalent system. It is important, however, to approach filtration with the proper attitude. In particular, it should not be seen as a cure for major problems that arise from technical errors in brewing. It will not successfully clarify and stabilize beers with excessive turbidity. Moreover, removal of microorganisms via a sterile filtration of 1 micron or less can ruin the malt character of the finished beer. This is particularly true of the Vienna recipes given in Chapter 3.

On the other hand, the benefits of a 3 micron polish filtration are numerous. There will be some yeast carried over, but of a very beneficial type, provided the beer is not exposed to elevated temperatures. In particular, there will be enough yeast passing through the filter (typically 100 to 200 cells per milliliter) to achieve the benefits of keeping the beer "alive" under proper conditions. Yet, the yeast sediment itself will be invisible to the naked eye.

There will also be a complete removal of residual yeasty/sulfury flavor tones. Virtually all of the dead and dormant yeast will be filtered out. In addition, the use of CO_2 to push the beer through the filter has its own benefits. In particular, allowing a slight gas bleed in the receiving tank will scrub out the remaining green beer volatiles in the transfer. It is of course important to purge the receiving tank with CO_2 before transfer to remove air.

While polish filtration has many attractive advantages, and at the margin does produce slightly better beers, it is not essential for the recipes in Chapter 3. As a general rule, amber beers are easier to clarify than their paler counterparts. This is because the amber malts tend naturally to promote a more favorable pH for large protein separation in both the mash and kettle boil than lighter malts. The use of top-quality Pilsener malt as the base malt enhances this effect. Also, a slight yeasty flavor tone is usually less distracting in amber beers than it is in pale beers.

CARBONATION

The presence of CO_2 tends to promote smoothness of beer flavor. Thus, it is a welcome addition to the Vienna flavor profile, but only up to a point. Excessive carbonation can lead to "bland" or "homogenized" flavors where some of the more delicate features of beer flavor—more notably those contributed by hop volatiles—are obscured. This robs Viennas of flavor complexity, something the authors feel distinguishes really top-flight versions from average ones.

The traditional recommendation for a wide range of continental style lagers is 2.4 to 2.6 volumes of CO_2 for the finished beer. This means that there are 2.4 to 2.6 liters of CO_2 per liter of beer. In European units this is equivalent to 0.465 to 0.508 grams of CO_2 per 100 grams of beer.

There are four basic ways to carbonate beer:

1. Bottle conditioning with a sugar prime
2. Bottle conditioning with a malt wort prime
3. Bulk kraeusen with malt wort, followed by counterpressure filling
4. Direct CO_2 injection followed by counterpressure filling

The test brews were carbonated using the authors' Zahm and Nagel unit. This can be used for either the third or fourth procedure. Actually, all that is needed is a tank that has a pressure gauge attached and a method for measuring the temperature inside. At equilibrium conditions the beer CO_2 level in volumes can be obtained from Table 2. For example, at 32 degrees F (0 degrees C) a pressure of 7 psi gives 2.38 volumes while 9 psi gives 2.59 volumes. At 38 degrees F (3.5 degrees C) these are increased to 10 psi and 12 psi, respectively.

For most of the ten-odd years the authors have been using their Zahm and Nagel system, the kraeusen procedure was used. It was an article of my faith that a "natural carbonation" would produce the best beer foam. This is simply not true. Direct CO_2 injection, hardly a "unnatural" procedure, can be very effective. The key is to obtain equilibrium conditions so that the data in Table 2 are valid.

Temperature is important. The closer one can get to 32 degrees F (0 degrees C), the more readily the beer absorbs CO_2 and reaches a proper pressure-temperature equilibrium. If necessary, the carbonating tank can be packed in ice. It is also important to purge the carbonating tank with CO_2 before transferring beer into it.

In the Zahm and Nagel system a small carbonating stone, sometimes called a diffuser, is attached to the gas line. This breaks up the CO_2 flow, and literally sprays small CO_2 bubbles into the beer. By gently rocking the tank during CO_2 feeds, one can obtain equilibrium conditions within one hour, provided the temperature is kept below 36 degrees F (2 degrees C). A 30 minute rest after equilibrium is achieved is desirable.

If CO_2 is directly injected through a gas line without diffusers, more time will be needed. The authors have found that the best results are obtained by initially bringing the pressure to the 18 to 22 psi range. Over the next few hours, the pressure will drop, as part of the CO_2 is absorbed into the beer and the other part occupies the tank headspace. Bleed the latter off and inject CO_2 a second time. Repeat this procedure over a few days until the pressure stabilizes and equilibrium is achieved.

There are some advantages to the third procedure— using a wort kraeusen with fresh yeast —to get the desired CO_2 buildup. With defective beers, especially those with elevated diacetyl levels at the fermentation end point, a

Pounds per square inch (psi)

°F	1	2	3	4	5	6	7	8	9	10	11	12	13	14	15	16	17	18	19	20	21	22	23	24	25	26	27	28	29	30
30	1.82	1.92	2.03	2.14	2.23	2.36	2.48	2.60	2.70	2.82	2.93	3.02																		
31	1.78	1.88	2.00	2.10	2.20	2.31	2.42	2.54	2.65	2.76	2.86	2.96																		
32	1.75	1.85	1.95	2.05	2.16	2.27	2.38	2.48	2.59	2.70	2.80	2.90	3.01																	
33		1.81	1.91	2.01	2.12	2.23	2.33	2.43	2.53	2.63	2.74	2.84	2.96																	
34		1.78	1.86	1.97	2.07	2.18	2.28	2.38	2.48	2.58	2.68	2.79	2.89	3.00																
35			1.83	1.93	2.03	2.14	2.24	2.34	2.43	2.52	2.62	2.73	2.83	2.93	3.02															
36			1.79	1.88	1.99	2.09	2.20	2.29	2.39	2.47	2.57	2.67	2.77	2.86	2.96															
37				1.84	1.94	2.04	2.15	2.24	2.34	2.42	2.52	2.62	2.72	2.80	2.90	3.00														
38				1.80	1.90	2.00	2.10	2.20	2.29	2.38	2.47	2.57	2.67	2.75	2.85	2.94														
39					1.86	1.96	2.05	2.15	2.25	2.34	2.43	2.52	2.61	2.70	2.80	2.89	2.98													
40					1.82	1.92	2.01	2.10	2.20	2.30	2.39	2.47	2.56	2.65	2.75	2.84	2.93	3.01												
41						1.87	1.97	2.06	2.16	2.25	2.35	2.43	2.52	2.60	2.70	2.79	2.87	2.96												
42						1.83	1.93	2.02	2.12	2.21	2.30	2.39	2.47	2.56	2.65	2.74	2.82	2.91	3.00											
43						1.80	1.90	1.99	2.08	2.17	2.25	2.34	2.43	2.51	2.60	2.69	2.78	2.86	2.94											
44							1.86	1.95	2.04	2.13	2.21	2.30	2.39	2.47	2.56	2.64	2.73	2.81	2.89	2.99										
45							1.82	1.91	2.00	2.08	2.17	2.25	2.34	2.42	2.51	2.60	2.68	2.77	2.84	2.94	3.02									
46								1.88	1.96	2.04	2.13	2.22	2.30	2.38	2.47	2.55	2.63	2.72	2.80	2.89	2.98									
47								1.84	1.92	2.00	2.09	2.18	2.25	2.34	2.42	2.50	2.59	2.67	2.75	2.84	2.93	3.02								
48								1.80	1.88	1.96	2.05	2.14	2.21	2.30	2.38	2.46	2.55	2.63	2.70	2.79	2.87	2.96								
49									1.85	1.93	2.01	2.10	2.18	2.25	2.34	2.42	2.50	2.58	2.66	2.75	2.83	2.91	2.99							
50									1.82	1.90	1.98	2.06	2.14	2.21	2.30	2.38	2.45	2.54	2.62	2.70	2.78	2.86	2.94							
51										1.87	1.95	2.03	2.10	2.18	2.25	2.34	2.41	2.49	2.58	2.65	2.73	2.81	2.89	3.02						
52										1.84	1.91	1.99	2.06	2.14	2.22	2.30	2.37	2.45	2.54	2.61	2.69	2.76	2.84	2.93	3.00					
53										1.80	1.88	1.96	2.03	2.10	2.18	2.26	2.33	2.41	2.48	2.57	2.65	2.72	2.80	2.88	2.95	3.03				
54											1.85	1.93	2.00	2.07	2.15	2.22	2.29	2.37	2.44	2.52	2.60	2.67	2.75	2.83	2.90	2.98				
55											1.82	1.89	1.97	2.04	2.11	2.19	2.25	2.33	2.40	2.47	2.57	2.63	2.70	2.78	2.85	2.93	3.01			
56												1.86	1.94	2.00	2.07	2.15	2.21	2.29	2.36	2.43	2.52	2.58	2.65	2.73	2.80	2.88	2.96			
57												1.83	1.90	1.97	2.04	2.11	2.18	2.25	2.33	2.40	2.47	2.54	2.61	2.69	2.76	2.84	2.91	2.99		
58												1.80	1.86	1.94	2.00	2.07	2.14	2.21	2.29	2.36	2.43	2.50	2.57	2.64	2.72	2.80	2.86	2.94	3.01	
59													1.80	1.90	1.97	2.04	2.11	2.18	2.25	2.32	2.39	2.46	2.53	2.60	2.67	2.75	2.81	2.89	2.96	3.03
60														1.87	1.94	2.01	2.08	2.14	2.21	2.28	2.35	2.42	2.49	2.56	2.63	2.70	2.77	2.84	2.91	2.98

Degrees Fahrenheit

Table 2: Volumes of Carbon Dioxide (CO_2).
© Byron Burch, Great Fermentations of Santa Rosa, 1991.

kraeusening can partially remedy problems in ways that extended aging cannot. In addition, this procedure usually will reduce the time required for cold storage. Certainly, if a brief two-week aging period is used, then a kraeusened beer will generally be superior to one carbonated by direct CO_2 injection.

In kraeusening, one adds more wort than is needed to achieve the desired CO_2 level. A 20 to 25 percent charge is traditional. As the second fermentation takes place, the excess CO_2 is bled off until the fermentation end point is obtained. The pressure is then reduced to its desired level by an additional CO_2 bleed. A good temperature to use for this process is 36 to 40 degrees F (2 to 4 degrees C).

In both the third and fourth procedures, one must take into account the desirable (and necessary) "foam-over" during the counterpressure fill. The authors' measurements indicate that a good foam-over can be achieved with a CO_2 loss of 0.1 to 0.2 volumes. Thus, if one is carbonating at 35 degrees F (2 degrees C), then one should shoot for an equilibrium pressure of 12 psi or 2.7 volumes. This will generally mean that the finished beer will end at 2.5 to 2.6 volumes after the fill.

The addition of sugar to beer bottles before filling has been long used to carbonate homebrew. It is unacceptably erratic for lagers that have aged any length of time. The primary reason is that the old yeast from the primary fermentation is usually not suitable for the second fermentation. Fresh yeast produces better results. Given the necessity of adding yeast, why not use regular wort and dispense with sugar additives?

Whenever there is spare time available, it is convenient to prepare a mini batch of priming wort, or wort to be used for the kraeusening procedure described above. After this wort is boiled it is transferred to clean beer bottles and pasteurized. The classic rule is to hold the bottles in a water bath at 140 degrees F (60 degrees C) for 20 minutes. Once this is done, the wort can be stored in a refrigerator. Any defects will be signalled by the development of turbidity, but this never should occur if pasteurization is done correctly. If this wort is kept too long it will deepen in color, at which point it should be discarded.

In the second procedure, bottle conditioning with wort, one combines some fresh yeast with the wort prime and allows it to start fermenting. When fermentation starts it is combined with the main batch and transferred to beer bottles. Since there is no opportunity to adjust pressure levels, an exact amount of priming wort needs to be used. The following rule, from reference 13, is reasonable.

$$\frac{V_P}{V_B} = \frac{SG_B}{SG_P} \times \frac{Cv}{2.44 \times SG_B \times G_P \times F - Cv}$$

Here

V_P = volume of priming solution to be added
V_B = volume of beer to be primed
SG_B = specific gravity of beer to be primed
SG_P = specific gravity of priming solution
F = fractional fermentability of priming solution
C_V = CO_2 level in volumes

For example, suppose the beer to be primed has a specific gravity of

$$SG_B = 1.010$$

Suppose the priming solution is 65 percent fermentable and so

$$F = 0.65$$

In addition, suppose the prime's extract gives

$$Gp = 12° \text{ P}, SGp = 1.048$$

Then, to achieve a CO_2 level of 2.5 volumes we need

$$\frac{V_P}{V_B} = \frac{1.010}{1.048} \times \frac{2.5}{2.44 \times 1.010 \times 12 \times .65 - 2.5}$$

$$= .144$$

Thus a 14.4 percent prime charge is needed, or 0.72 gallons for a 5 gallon batch.

SANITATION

By necessity, this book has focused on issues which separate Viennese beers from other styles—recipes, brewing materials and procedures. Yet all these matters pale in significane in comparison with sanitation (and also the proper care of yeast).

For Viennas (and indeed for any colored beers) sanitation is a double-edged issue. It is clearly important that the equipment used be properly cleaned and sterilized. But it is also important that residual chemicals used in sanitation be completely removed from the equipment because amber and dark beers are excellent absorbants, due to their polarity and viscosity (reference 9). Absorbancy is an issue for pale beers, but it is particularly important for colored beers. The flavor tones in beer that develop from residual chemicals can be quite strange, and are often thought (wrongly) to be from bacterial infection.

The procedure described below was used for the test brews associated with this book. The author's brewing equipment is stainless steel, including mash-tun, brew kettle, fermenters, and storage tanks. The procedures reflects this, and obvious modifications are needed for items such as glass carboys.

After use, there is a hot water pre-rinse to remove bulk dirt (proteins, yeast, etc.) This is followed by a hot water wash until the equipment is visually clean. The final cleaning step consists of the traditional procedure described by deClerck (reference 7). Here the equipment is filled with very hot water (170 degrees F [77 degrees C] or hotter) and a cleaner for an 8 to 12 hour period. Because of the extended contact period, chlorinated products should be avoided since they are aggressive even to high quality stainless steel. A favorite cleaner is TSP (trisodium phosphate), but other alternatives exist.

After cleaning, the equipment should be rinsed with hot water, and then they are ready for sterilization. Iodophors (1.75 percent iodine, 18.75 percent phosphoric acids) are very effective for a wide range of materials including most metals. This is the sanitizer used by the authors for the test brews. Peracidic acid (acetic acid plus hydrogen peroxide) is very popular in Europe and is starting to be used in the U.S. It possibly is worth our attention. Both of these are rated as "no rinse required," and hence the equipment can be stored after the sanitizer is removed.

Rinsing is advised before the equipment is re-used. For this, nothing beats sterile beer, and in this regard, cheap "supermarket" commercial beer is recommended. (Why waste our own!). Twelve ounces is sufficient for a 5 gallon container, and this should be increased or decreased in proportion to the volume of the vessel that is to be rinsed.

QUALITY CONTROL

Given the expense of the materials used in Vienna-style beers, it is worthwhile to have some sort of quality control program. A number of options are pointed out in reference 24. Two of these were found particularly useful in preparing the brews for this book. They are the following:

Wort Stability Test—Just after wort is chilled and aerated, and just before the yeast is pitched, transfer 100 to 500 milliliter of wort to a sterile beer bottle. Plug the bottle with cotton and hold at 86 degrees F (30 degrees C) for at least 72 hours. This sample should remain stable (i.e., free of turbidity and bacterial activity).

Originally, this test was designed to identify possible wort spoilage. However, its real value is more general. If one cannot deliver wort to the fermenter which passes this test, then something is fundamentally wrong with the sanitation procedure. This test also reminds us that proper sanitation is very much of a "what have you done for me lately" type of issue. Sometimes even accomplished brewers need their bell rung, and this test will do just that.

The second test was originally proposed by Rodney Morris to evaluate yeast. It is particularly useful for brewers who reuse yeast, as it is capable of detecting disorders at very low levels, well before they are relevant to the finished beer. Thus, one has some time either to harvest new yeast or purchase a new supply. The test is also useful for those who do not reuse yeast. Indeed, if there are flavor disorders in the finished beer, then this test will indicate whether these are due to the yeast pitched.

Morris Yeast Test—Prepare 500 ml of unhopped wort. This can be done while brewing. Boil this wort for 30 minutes, and cool to 68 degrees F (20 degrees C). Combine some yeast (5 grams of a slurry is fine), and the chilled wort in a suitable container. Aerate and ferment, holding the temperature at 68 degrees F (20 degrees C). When this is completed, decant the wort off the yeast sediment and store at 50 degrees F (10 degrees C) for three days. It is best to fill the jar full with a minimum head space to avoid air pickup. At the end of storage, decant again and carefully taste. Buttery/diacetyl flavors (taste and smell) indicate yeast mutation and/or bacterial infection. Sulfury flavors are a sure indication of an infection, while phenolic tones point to the presence of wild yeast. If these defects are at low levels, then they will not be detectable in the main batch fermented normally with the yeast. This, of course, is why Morris's test is so practical.

The authors have also been using HLP, a media that can be obtained from Siebels in Chicago. Teri Fahrendorf has an excellent article on this media (reference 25), which should be consulted for details. The reader should be warned that this media has a terrible reputation with industrial microbiologists because it contains sulfites. The latter have been added to create anaerobic conditions needed in the detection of lactobacillus and pediococcus. The sulfites and the anaerobic conditions will zap practically all aerobic and partially anaerobic bacteria. Thus, claims in Siebel's instructions that this is a general media are questionable. The sulfites do nothing for the lactos and pedios, but some can survive and will be detected if present in sufficiently large concentrations.

In spite of all these limitations, the authors agree with Teri that it is a highly practical media for homebrewers and brew pubs. It is very easy to prepare (and in fact similar to an elementary "homebrew kit" for beginners), and the bacteria can be indentified visually (a microscope is not needed). While it will undercount the lactos and pedios, nevertheless if they do not show up in the HLP tubes, experience has shown that they are at a low enough concentration that the yeast tested can be used without danger of off flavors. It is important to maintain 30° C (85° F) during incubation. Teri has described an imaginative incubator in her article. The authors have used a water bath with an aquarium heater.

Testing with HLP is compatible with the Morris test since taking samples from the forced fermentation usually gives the most accurate results. It is also important to sample yeast that have been kept in storage, since lactos and pedios can grow from small and insignificant concentrations in this period to a point where they are highly relevant.

Appendix A

Commercial Examples

Perhaps the most authentic of the Viennese-style beers brewed commercially are to be found in Bavaria during the Oktoberfest. As noted earlier, it was indeed the Bavarians who kept the Dreher tradition alive in Europe. The authors have had the good fortune of being in Bavaria on four different occasions in October, and have taken full advantage of these opportunities to enjoy the beers available at that time. What is truly impressive is the care and attention the breweries give to these beers, both the large and small breweries. The extended aging period is the rule rather than the exception, and the average beer quality is very high. As the Narziss article (reference 3) indicates, the starting gravity of these beers falls in the range 1.051 to 1.055 (12.5° to 13.5° P), so these amount to authentically produced standard Viennas of Dreher's time.

The big Munich breweries go all-out for this festival. The standard and long-time champion of this style is the Späten brewery. Their Ur-Märzen justly deserves the praise that has been given to it. It is a marvelous beer. Equally outstanding is the Märzen produced by Hofbräuhaus. Both these beers are smooth with rounded flavors which display

75

a beautiful malt character. Another beer of interest is the Märzen Bier produced by Paulaner. While it has always been overshadowed by this brewery's classic Salvator, it certainly needs no apologies. This brewery also produces a bottled Oktoberfest year round, and this is exported to the U.S. The authors have seen two versions. One is packaged in small green bottles, and in Texas these have the "malt liquor" appellation conspicuously missing from the label, which means it is under 4 percent alcohol by weight. This is reflected in the flavors, and it is more of a "German mild" than Oktoberfest. The other version is marketed in brown Euro-bottles and does have "malt liquor" stamped on its label. Thus it is definitely above 4 percent. When fresh it would make an excellent standard for judges of the Vienna/Oktoberfest/Märzen category in competitions. The light amber color of this beer is right on the mark.

The author's favorite festival beers are made in Kulmbach, an historic brewing center. There are four breweries located here, namely EKU (Erste Kulmbacher Actienbrauerei), Monchshof-Brau, Reichelbrau, and Sandlerbrau. All of these breweries produce Oktoberfest/Märzen beer, which is typically called Festbier. They all share an exceptional malt character which has considerable elegance and finesse. EKU produces a bottled Oktoberfest which is exported to the U.S. When fresh, it would make a very good standard for judges in competitions. Its color, however, is at the lighter end of the acceptable range for this beer style.

Beers with the term Märzen on the label are still brewed in Austria, the term "Märzen" as well as the term "spezial" being used for brews of the export type. The Brau AG Märzen, brewed at Lenz, is typical. It has an original gravity of 1.048 (12.1° P), a strength 4.06 percent by weight, and an IBU of 21. It has a color of 7.6° EBC, which is straw yellow without the slightest hint of amber. A fine export it is, a traditional Märzen it is not.

Michael Jackson (reference 15) has reported that an authentic Vienna was brewed in 1987 to celebrate the 150th anniversary of the Ottakringer Brewery, called Ottakringer 150 Jahre. The authors have not had the privilege of tasting this brew, but from Jackson's description, it seems to be very much the real thing. The description included " . . . a full, reddish bronze color (25° EBC), a malty aroma, a lightly sweet, soft start, and a dry rounded finish . . ." There can be no doubt that a beer like this would do well in the U. S. import market.

One of the authors became familiar with Viennese-style beers during his undergraduate days from those brewed in Mexico. At Christmas break, it became customary for groups to head south to Orizaba for a few days, where the first batches of Noche Bueno became available. This beer was brewed only for the Christmas season, and was a standard for many of us for character and flavor not to be found in beers brewed north of the Rio Grande. Mexican beers have always been unique. The pale beers, invariably lagers, generally have an exceptionally dry finish, which combined with a slight thinness makes them seem hoppier than their actual IBUs would indicate. Characteristics like this are completely compatible with Mexico's climate and cuisine. With the ambers, the dryness and hoppy character-istics are retained, but the thinness is replaced with rounded malt tones. Thus, they are quintessentially Viennese in overall terms.

Noche Bueno is arguably Mexico's finest beer. At 12° L, it is on the dark side for a Vienna, but this is consistent with the Graf version of this style. The recipe in Chapter 3 for this version is based on Noche Bueno. According to the author's calculation and measurements, Noche Bueno has a strength of 4.1 to 4.25 percent by weight, and an original gravity of 1.055 to 1.057 (3.5° to 14.0° P). These figures differ somewhat from figures quoted elsewhere (references 14 and 15), which in turn differ from each other. Information sources at Orizaba are not always reliable.

Noche Bueno is brewed by the Moctequma group headquartered in Mexico City. It is one of the three major Mexican brewing organizations, and has had in the last few decades the strongest commitment to Viennese style beers. They also brew lighter colored ambers similar to the first recipe in Chapter 3. Outstanding is the Tres Equis Oscura (XXX Oscura). A much lighter-flavored beer called Sol Oscura is also interesting. However, the amber lager that is best known to North Americans from this group is Dos Equis (XX). It is important to stress that this beer has always been formulated with the North American market in mind, and lacks the character of the beers cited above. It can be best described as a "mild," not dissimilar from Shiner's Bock, Yuengling's Porter, and Michelob's Classic Dark. Dos Equis is not a bad beer, and indeed finds application with certain meals and social occasions. Nevertheless, it makes as much sense to use it as a standard for the Vienna category in competitions as it does to use Miller Lite as the standard for Pilseners.

The Modelo group, also headquartered in Mexico City but with breweries at various locations, is the largest brewing organization in Mexico. They brew an excellent Graf-style Vienna called Negra Modelo. It is somewhat lighter in flavor than Noche Bueno, but when fresh it has an exceptionally smooth finish. Many consider it to be very much Noche Bueno's equal. Exactly the same beer is marketed under the Negra Leon label, and both brands are available year-round.

The Cuauhtemoc group, headquartered in Monterrey,

Dan Fink

is the last of the big three. They concentrate almost exclusively on pale lagers, and many feel their Bohemia to be Mexico's best premium Pilsener. A thin amber-colored beer called Indio is sometimes brewed, but it lacks the character of this group's pale beers. It also suffers in comparison with the ambers cited above.

This group operates the old Graf brewery at Toluca. Sadly, only two common pale lagers are brewed there. However, the plant itself is a credit to the firm, for it is a modern facility with a capacity in excess of four million barrels. The Cuauhtemoc group has been cited, along with other Monterrey-based industries, as a model industry for developing countries because of its willingness to re-invest profits for modernization. As impressive as this is, the Mexican brewing industry still suffers from failure to invest properly in research, and establish a strong "in-house" brewing science base. This is most clearly seen in less than impressive brewhouse procedures. All of the problems related to wort production cited in Chapter 4 are common. As a result, the shelf life of Mexican beers is typically limited. The pale lagers tend to develop distracting metallic tones. This development is even worse in the ambers, which can become downright unpleasant. Noche Bueno, for example, has always been hopelessly unstable as a bottled beer under trade conditions. Others fare better, but it is rare in North America to find one in truly peak condition.

Another concern about Mexican brewing is the so-called "Corona effect." Brewers overreacted to the temporary popularity of this beer, thinking it to be the beer of the 1990s. In fact it is what it always has been, namely an inexpensive common beer. The consequences have not been happy. Noche Bueno was not brewed in 1990 nor 1991, and production of Tres Equis Oscura has been terminated. Presumably these have been considered passé as the brewery looks for a Corona look-alike. The list goes on, but now that the Corona bubble has burst, maybe Mexican breweries can come to their senses and go back to doing those things they do well. This includes (among other things) producing ambers with character and substance.

The trends north of the border are in a different direction in breweries of virtually all sizes. A major step forward was taken when Coors decided to market its Winterfest, at least on a seasonal basis. A winner in the 1990 Great American Beer Festival in the Vienna category, it is in the authors' view the best beer brewed by a large national brewery in the U.S. If one had any doubts about the Moravian III strain of barley used by Coors being an authentic "Pilsener type," they will be entirely removed by this beer. Fred Eckhardt has given the following profile for Winterfest: Original gravity = 1.066 (16° P), alcohol = 4.5 percent by weight, color = 4° L, IBU = 17. This is the type of beer the authors remember tasting in Golden, Colorado before Winterfest was distributed on the open market. The current product seems to be lighter in body and flavor, but the elegance of the malt character is very much there. Beers like this will never have a sales volume and market share that will impress accountants. But what they will do is to give the brewery a measure of respect that is not attainable in other ways. In the end, this cannot help but do good things for the sales volume and market share of the breweries' other product lines.

Anheuser Busch is producing a beer called "Anheuser" which is being promoted as a "Märzen beer." This term should be interpreted in the sense that it is currently being used in Austria, namely as another name for an export style beer. It is clean and well balanced. A fine export indeed, but different in character from the traditional Märzen described in this book.

The situation is even brighter with the middle-sized regionals. The Pittsburgh Brewing Company has a long and glorious tradition with amber and dark colored lagers. However, their management has always seemed embarrassed by beers of this type. In the early 1980s they introduced a world class Münchner called I.C. Dark, which died in obscurity in spite of critical praise. Their most recent effort, possibly their best, is an Oktoberfest brewed under contract for Jim Koch and the Boston Beer Company. Even for hop freaks, it is at the outer limits in hop bitterness for the Vienna style, yet it works. There is in fact a remarkable synergism between the hop flavor and the fruity, sulfury, very slightly phenolic character that is found in all of Pittsburgh's beers. This is a serious brew of considerable complexity. Much has been said, pro and con, about contract brewing. However, if these folks do nothing else other than getting these old breweries back to brewing beers that make sense in terms of their intrinsic capabilities and characteristics—and not slavishly copying whatever the big boys are doing—then whatever indiscretions the contractors make along the way can be readily forgiven. A big plus for this particular Oktoberfest is that it will be marketed by Koch's organization, which means it will not be neglected, but rather will be promoted with intelligence and vigor. This very substantial brew deserves no less.

Another regionally-produced Oktoberfest of merit is made by the Dixie Brewing Company in New Orleans. It is now become traditional to launch the Dixie Cup homebrew competition held each October in Houston by tapping a keg of the Dixie seasonal. The fact that the production staff at Dixie are all enthusiastic homebrewers only adds to the ambiance of the occasion. This is a superb beer, and the authors only hope that the fine citizens of New Orleans realize what a gem they have in their local brewery.

The best example of the Graf version currently available is the Oktoberfest brewed by the August Schell Brewing Company of New Ulm, Minn. It has a reddish copper color,

Dan Fink

a bit lighter than Noche Bueno or Negra Modelo, but no less full in body and texture. The subtle yet positive flavor tone coming from black malts is exactly what one looks for in this type of amber lager. It is also a well-made beer. The authors received samples through the mail, where they were probably abused during transit. Any such abuse was not reflected in the beer's flavor, a good sign that proper care has been taken in brewing, and in particular the brewhouse. The folks at New Ulm do good work indeed!

The authors have not been able to determine the type

of malt used for August Schell's amber. However, beer flavors indicate that a good deal of six-row malt was used, and indeed the brew could conceivably have been made exclusively from six-row malt. This brings out a point that the authors have seen in other beer styles, and adds an extra dimension to the two-row versus six-row issue. While choice of the barley variety is quite important, it nevertheless, must yield to the importance of brewhouse procedure in overall consideration.

A light-colored amber called Pecan Street is currently being brewed at New Ulm under a contract with the Old City Brewing Co. in Austin, Texas. Previously it was brewed by Shiner, and it is mainly marketed in Texas. Pecan Street is a very nice beer, but lacks the body and character of a traditional Vienna. It is, however, by a wide margin the best example of a "Vienna mild," exceeding even European "milds" in overall quality.

It is fitting that there are a number of Vienna-style lagers being brewed by microbrewers. These people along with their comrades in the homebrewing community have been largely responsible for resurrecting this style. One of the first, and many argue the best, is Ambier by Gary Bauer. Technically, this is a contract beer, but not in the usual sense of a promoter putting his or her name and label on a beer brewed by someone else. Whenever it is time to brew a batch of Ambier, you can bet Gary will be on hand supervising the operations. His impeccable standards in the area of wort production are seen in this beer. In fact, Ambier makes the reverse point made by Noche Bueno, namely that a well-made amber can have incredible flavor stability. The authors have tasted samples of Ambier on a number of occasions which have been in 12-ounce bottles for nine months or more. Never once did they given any indication of their actual age.

Another early microbrewed amber lager of distinction is the one produced by Abita of Abita Springs, La. The spring water used by the brewery has an abnormally high sulfur content. While this may not be suited to all beer styles, it works three times over for their amber. Direct comparison with Ambier shows the latter to be slightly cleaner and a bit more rounded in flavor. The Abita amber is, however, the more complex brew. Actually, comparisons are not really meaningful for they represent two different ways to do an amber. The beer world is a richer place that both are out there.

The authors have heard glowing reports about the Oktoberfest brewed at Helen, Georgia by the Friends Brewing Company. Demand for this beer has reached the point that the brewery has started producing it year-round. There are undoubtedly many other microbrewed ambers that are unknown to the authors.

The early brewpubs tended to be oriented to top fermented ales, but the late 1980s has seen the emergence of lager brewpubs. A notable example is Pennsylvania Brewing Co./Allegheny Brewery and Pub founded by Tom Pastorius in Pittsburgh, Penn. It is indeed a model for this type of operation. The restaurant is immaculately clean, and tastefully done in a German motif. The brewhouse, visible to the customers, is spacious, well laid out, and contains new copper vessels imported from Germany. This brewpub started with two pale lagers, a hoppy Pilsener and a slightly sweet Helles style beer, as well as a dark beer. An amber Oktoberfest has recently been introduced, and the version tasted by the authors in the Spring of 1991 was dead on the mark. It recalls Gary Bauer's Vienna in its overall quality, and the brewpub reports that sales of this beer are quite strong. A real class act here.

The authors have not had the opportunity to visit the

brewpub in Los Angeles operated by the famous chef, Wolfgang Puck. However, reports have been glowing. Apparently, amber-colored festival beers will be brewed on a seasonal basis, and they, like everything else associated with this operation, will undoubtedly be of a high quality.

The story does not end here, a number of groups are about to start lager brewpubs and this includes none other than Dave Miller. That Viennese-style beers will find their way into the product mix, at least on a seasonal basis, seems certain, given their commercial success in other operations. It is for this and other reasons that one can feel very optimistic about the future of lagers with a Viennese character.

Appendix B

BEER COLOR

The classic color unit of Lovibond degrees is the one chosen for this book. The following is the standard verbal description of this unit.

Basic Color	Hue	°L
Yellow	Light	0 – 2.5
	Pale	2.5 – 3.5
	Deep straw/gold	3.5 – 5.5
Amber	Light	5.5 – 8
	Medium	8 – 10
	Deep	10 – 14
Dark	Brown/black	14 – 18
	Black	above 18

Many authors recommend using the malt color rating to predict beer color. See for example Byron Burch's article in reference 16. Suppose we are using 8.5 pounds of a pale malt rated at 1.8° L in a five-gallon batch. This would be projected to give

$$8.5 \times 1.8 = 15.3° \text{L}$$

in a five gallon batch or

$$15.3° \text{ L per 5 gallons} = 3.06° \text{ L per gallon.}$$

3.06° L is the estimate of the finished beer color. For pale beers approximations like this are usually reasonable. For amber colored beers they typically are not. For example, a standard Vienna formulation would have 7.5 pounds of a pale malt at 1.8° L and 9 ounces of colored malts at 20° L in a five-gallon batch. This projects to the following:

$$
\begin{array}{rcll}
7.5 & \times & 1.8 & = \quad 13.5 \\
9/16 & \times & 20 & = \quad \underline{11.25} \\
& & & \quad 24.75° \text{ L}
\end{array}
$$

Normalizing we would predict

$$\frac{25.75}{5} = 5.15° \text{ L}$$

as the final beer color. In reality this beer is typically in the 8° to 10° L range. The reason why the estimates are so bad is that color does not develop on a proportional basis except for very light-colored beers. As a consequence, only empirical methods are capable of giving reliable results.

The following is an empirical procedure developed by the author and Roger Briess. It can be applied directly to a finished beer. For formulation, one needs to brew a small batch and test the clarified wort obtained from that.

The standard for this test is Michelob Classic Dark. The reason is that it is widely available, and its color is known (17° L). The test consists of diluting the standard with water until a color match with the sample is obtained. Figure 1 gives the relationship between the amount of water added and the degrees Lovibond of the sample.

MATERIALS NEEDED

1. Distilled water—Colored tap water can increase the errors in this test from 1 percent to 10 or 20 percent.

2. Blender—Dissolved CO_2 in beer will affect its color. Both the standard and sample should be degassed. This can be done in a blender. A lot of foam will be created, but once it recedes and the beer falls clear it is ready for testing.

3. Light source—It is important for the visual comparison to take place in a well-lit environment. Ideally, this consists of a lamp with a 100-watt bulb against a white background. Be sure to use the reflected rather than direct light, and place the samples the same distance from the light source. Also, take time in making the comparison because the difference in one or two degrees Lovibond is not that great.

4. Vessels—These are the most important components to this test. After extensive experimentation it became clear that two sets are needed. For detailed testing, two glass jars of one-inch diameter and a capacity of at 125 milliliters are best. For samples below 10° L the volume of these vessels is not large enough. Two clear 12-ounce export (long neck) returnable bottles will be needed. The Miller Brewing Co. has been using these bottles. So has Corona, but the label, which cannot be removed, is a distraction.

5. Syringe—This is needed to measure 10 cc (10 milliliters) of water.

PROCEDURE

1. Clean everything
2. De-gas the beers in blender
3. Measure 20 mL of standard beer into export bottle No. 1.
4. Measure 20 mL of sample beer into export bottle No. 2.
5. If colors are different, measure 10 mL of distilled water into bottle No. 1 and 10 mL of sample beer into export bottle No. 2.
6. Continue Step 5 until colors become close. At this point the comparisons should be made in the one inch diameter jars. Transfer 25 to 50 mL into these from the export bottles and return after comparison. Cut the water and sample beer increment from 10 mL to 5 mL.
7. When a color match is obtained, record the total amount of water added. Figure 1 gives the associated degrees Lovibond.

EXAMPLE—BASS PALE ALE

The Bass ale is selected for this example since it is in the middle of the desirable color range for Viennas (i.e., 10° L), and widely available. At the start the 20 mL of standard beer (Michelob Classic Dark) will be discernibly darker than the sample (Bass). After adding 30 mL of water to the standard, the colors will become close, and at this point the one-inch jars are needed. A match is obtained after an additional 10 ml of water is added. Thus a total of 40 mL of water was needed, and from Figure 1, we see that Bass has a color of

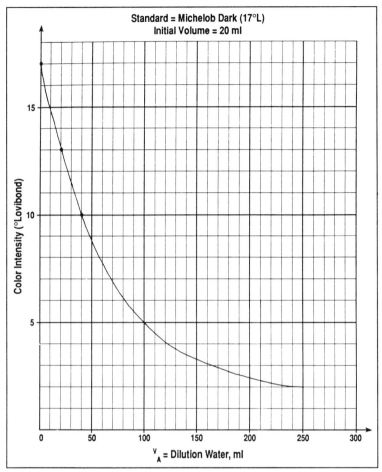

Standard = Michelob Dark (17°L)
Initial Volume = 20 ml

Color Intensity (°Lovibond)

V_A = Dilution Water, ml

Figure 1: Intensity/Dilution Chart

10° L. Since only 60 mL of liquid was used in each bottle, the entire test could have been done in the one-inch diameter jars.

Note that the relationship between degrees Lovibond and dilution water is not linear. For example, adding 20 mL of water to 20 mL of Michelob Classic Dark (17° L) will not cut the color in half. In fact, instead of 17/2 = 8.5° L the color will be higher, namely 13° L (see Figure 1). This lack of proportionality is why the relationship between degrees Lovibond and degrees EBC can be in error. It also explains why beer color and malt color are not proportional.

At the lower color range, on the other hand, proportionality is approximately valid. Thus, diluting 20 mL of Molson Export Ale (4° L) with 20 ml of water will give a color very close to Budweiser (2° L). However, once one gets into the color range relevant to Viennas, rules based on proportionality are impractical.

Glossary

adjunct. Any *unmalted* grain or other fermentable ingredient added to the mash.

aeration. The action of introducing air to the wort at various stages of the brewing process.

airlock. (see fermentation lock)

airspace. (see ullage)

alcohol by volume (v/v). The percentage of volume of alcohol per volume of beer. To calculate the approximate volumetric alcohol content, subtract the terminal gravity from the original gravity and divide the result by 75. For example: 1.050 - 1.012 = .038 / 75 = 5% v/v.

alcohol by weight (w/v). The percentage weight of alcohol per volume of beer. For example: 3.2% alcohol by weight = 3.2 grams of alcohol per 100 centiliters of beer.

ale. 1. Historically, an unhopped malt beverage. 2. Now a generic term for hopped beers produced by top fermentation, as opposed to lagers, which are produced by bottom fermentation.

all-extract beer. A beer made with only malt extract as opposed to one made from barley, or a combination of malt extract and barley.

all-grain beer. A beer made with only malted barley as opposed to one made from malt extract, or from malt extract and malted barley.

all-malt beer. A beer made with only barley malt with no adjuncts or refined sugars.

alpha acid. A soft resin in hop cones. When boiled, alpha acids are converted to iso-alpha-acids, which account for 60 percent of a beer's bitterness.

alpha-acid unit. A measurement of the potential bitterness of hops, expressed by their percentage of alpha acid. Low = 2 to 4%, medium = 5 to 7%, high = 8 to 12%. Abbrev: A.A.U.

apparent extract. This measure in gravity units is the ratio of the weight of the fermented beer to an equivalent volume of water. It does not reflect the gravity of the residual extract left at the end of fermentation since fermented beer consists mainly of residual extract, water, and alcohol. The latter weigh less than water. See real extract.

Balling. A saccharometer invented by Carl Joseph Napoleon Balling in 1843. It is calibrated for 63.5 degrees F (17.5 degrees C), and graduated in grams per hundred, giving a direct reading of the percentage of extract by weight per 100 grams solution. For example: 10 °B = 10 grams of sugar per 100 grams of wort.

carbonation. The process of introducing carbon-dioxide gas into a liquid by: 1. injecting the finished beer with carbon dioxide; 2. adding young fermenting beer to finished beer for a renewed fermentation (kraeusening); 3. priming (adding sugar) to fermented wort prior to bottling, creating a secondary fermentation in the bottle.

carboy. A large glass, plastic or earthenware bottle.

chill haze. Haziness caused by protein and tannin during the secondary fermentation.

dry malt. Malt extract in powdered form.

extract. The amount of dissolved materials in the wort after mashing and lautering malted barley and/or malt adjuncts such as corn and rice.

fermentation lock. A one-way valve, which allows carbon-dioxide gas to escape from the fermenter while excluding contaminants.

final specific gravity. The specific gravity of a beer when fermentation is complete.

fining. The process of adding clarifying agents to beer during secondary fermentation to precipitate suspended matter.

flocculation. The behavior of yeast cells joining into masses and settling out toward the end of fermentation.

homebrew bittering units. A formula invented by the American Homebrewers Association to measure bitterness of beer. Example: 1.5 ounces of hops at 10 percent alpha acid for five gallons: 1.5 x 10 = 15 HBU per five gallons.

hop pellets. Finely powdered hop cones compressed into tablets. Hop pellets are 20 to 30 percent more bitter by weight than the same variety in loose form.

hydrometer. A glass instrument used to measure the specific gravity of liquids as compared to water, consisting of a graduated stem resting on a weighed float.

International bitterness units. This is an empirical quantity which was originally designed to measure the concentration of iso-alpha-acids in milligrams per liter (parts per million). Most procedures will also measure a small amount of uncharacterized soft resins so IBUs are generally 5 to 10% higher than iso-alpha acid concentrations.

kraeusen. (n.) The rocky head of foam which appears on the surface of the wort during fermentation. (v.) To add fermenting wort to fermented beer to induce carbonation through a secondary fermentation.

lager. (n.) A generic term for any bottom-fermented beer. Lager brewing is now the predominant brewing method worldwide except in Britain where top fermented ales dominate. (v.) To store beer at near-zero temperatures in order to precipitate yeast cells and proteins and improve taste.

lauter tun. A vessel in which the mash settles and the grains are removed from the sweet wort through a straining process. It has a false, slotted bottom and spigot.

malt. Barley that has been steeped in water, germinated, then dried in kilns. This process converts insoluble starchs to soluble substances and sugars.

malt extract. A thick syrup or dry powder prepared from malt.

Märzen. Beer brewed in March and stored during the summer months in caves. It became closely associated with Oktoberfest celebrations and such beers are often called Märzen/Oktoberfest.

mashing. Mixing ground malt with water to extract the fermentables, degrade haze-forming proteins and convert grain starches to fermentable sugars and nonfermentable carbohydrates.

modification. 1. The physical and chemical changes in barley as a result of malting. 2. The degree to which these changes have occured, as determined by the growth of the acrospire.

Oktoberfest. See Märzen.

original extract. This is the concentration of extract, fermentable and nonfermentable, that is present in wort at the start of the fermentation. It is measured both in gravity units, ratio of the weight of wort to an equivalent volume of wort, or as percent Balling or Plato. The latter is the grams of extract per 100 grams of wort.

original gravity. The specific gravity of wort previous to fermentation. A measure of the total amount of dissolved solids in wort.

oscura. A name used in Latin American beers which have an amber hue. Beers which fall into the deep gold/light amber are sometimes called semi-oscura.

pH. A measure of acidity or alkalinity of a solution, usually on a scale of one to 14, where seven is neutral.

Plato. A saccharometer that expresses specific gravity as extract weight in a one-hundred-gram solution at 68 degrees F (20 degrees C). A revised, more accurate version of Balling, developed by Dr. Plato.

primary fermentation. The first stage of fermentation, during which most fermentable sugars are converted to ethyl alcohol and carbon dioxide.

priming sugar. A small amount of corn, malt or cane sugar added to bulk beer prior to racking or at bottling to induce a new fermentation and create carbonation.

racking. The process of transferring beer from one container to another, especially into the final package (bottles, kegs, etc.).

real extract. This is the gravity of the actual residual extract in fermented beer. It can be measured with a hydrometer by first boiling off the alcohol in fermented beer, and replacing the volume lost with distilled water.

saccharometer. An instrument that determines the sugar concentration of a solution by measuring the specific gravity.

secondary fermentation. 1. The second, slower stage of fermentation, lasting from a few weeks to many months depending on the type of beer. 2. A fermentation occuring in bottles or casks and initiated by priming or by adding yeast.

sparging. Spraying the spent grains in the mash with hot water to retrieve the remaining malt sugar.

specific gravity. A measure of a substance's density as compared to that of water, which is given the value of 1.000 at 39.2 degrees F (4 degrees C). Specific gravity has no accompanying units, because it is expressed as a ratio.

starter. A batch of fermenting yeast, added to the wort to initiate fermentation.

strike temperature. The initial temperature of the water when the malted barley is added to it to create the mash.

trub. Suspended particles resulting from the precipitation of proteins, hop oils and tannins during boiling and cooling stages of brewing.

ullage. The empty space between a liquid and the top of its container. Also called airspace or headspace.

v/v: (see alcohol by volume)

w/v: (see alcohol by weight)

water hardness. The degree of dissolved minerals in water.

wort. The mixture that results from mashing the malt and boiling the hops, before it is fermented into beer.

Index

Bibliography

LISTED BY NUMBER

1. *One Hundred Years of Brewing*, Arno Press, New York, 1974.

2. A. Zimmermann, *Brauereibe briebslehre*, Buffalo, New York, 1904.

3. L. Narziss, "Bottom-fermentation special beers and their characteristics," *Brauwelt International*, 1985.

4. D. Bull, et. al., *American Breweries*, Bullworks, Trumbull, Connecticut, 1984.

5. F. Eckhardt, *A Treatise on Lager Beers*, Amateur Brewer, 1977.

6. Nugy, *Brewers Manual*, Jersey Printing, 1948.

7. J. deClerck, *A Textbook of Brewing*, Vol. 2, Chapman-Hall, 1957.

8. T. Foster, *Pale Ale*, Brewers Publications, 1990.

9. G. Fix, *Principles of Brewing Science*, Brewers Publications, 1989.

10. D. Miller, *Continental Pilsener*, Brewers Publications, 1990.

11. K. Oloff and A. Piendl, "Conventional Properties of Several Malt Types," *Brewers Digest*, 1978.

12. G. Fix, "Yeast," *Beer and Brewing*, Vol. 7, Brewers Publications, 1987.

13. G. Fix, "Beer Carbonation," *The New Brewer*, 1987.

14. F. Eckhardt, *The Essentials of Beer Style*, ABRIS, 1989.

15. M. Jackson, *Pocket Guide to Beer*, Simon and Schuster, 1988.

16. B. Byrch, "Recipe Formulation," *Beer and Brewing*, Vol. 7, Brewers Publications, 1987.

17. M. Jackson, *The World Guide to Beer*, The Running Press, Philadelphia, 1988.

18. R. Wahl and M. Henius, *American Handy Book of the Brewing, Malting, and Auxiliary Trades*, 2 vols., Wahl Henius Institute of Chicago, 1908.

19. M. Hennech, *Encyclopedia of Texas Breweries* (1836-1918), Ale Publications, Irving, Texas, 1990.

20. H. M. Broderick (ed.) *The Practical Brewer*, MBAA, 1977.

21. *The American Brewers Review*, Vol. 22, 1908.

22. D. Miller, *The Complete Handbook of Home Brewing*, Garden Way Publishing, 1988.

23. D. Miller, "Recipe Formulation," *Beer and Brewing,* Vol. 10, Brewers Publications, 1990.

24. G. Fix, "Simplified Quality Control," *Beer and Brewing,* Vol. 10, Brewers Publications, 1990.

25. T. Fahrendorf, "Home Lab Culturing", *Beer and Brewing,* Vol. 10, *Beer and Brewing,* Vol. 10, Brewers Publications, 1990.

26. J.E. Thausing, *The Theory and practice of the Preparation of Malt and the fabrication with Especial Reference to the Vienna Process of Brewing,* Henry Carey Baird and Company, London, 1882.

LISTED BY AUTHOR

The American Brewers Review, Vol. 22, 1908. (21)

H. M. Broderick (ed.) *The Practical Brewer,* MBAA, 1977. (20)

D. Bull, et. al., *American Breweries,* Bullworks, Trumbull, Connecticut, 1984. (4)

B. Byrch, "Recipe Formulation," *Beer and Brewing,* Vol. 7, Brewers Publications, 1987. (16)

J. deClerck, *A Textbook of Brewing,* Vol. 2, Chapman-Hall, 1957. (7)

F. Eckhardt, *The Essentials of Beer Style,* ABRIS, 1989. (14)

F. Eckhardt, *A Treatise on Lager Beers,* Amateur Brewer, 1977. (5)

T. Fahrendorf, "Home Lab Culturing", *Beer and Brewing,* Vol. 10, *Beer and Brewing,* Vol. 10, Brewers Publications, 1990.

G. Fix, "Beer Carbonation," *The New Brewer*, 1987. (13)

G. Fix, *Principles of Brewing Science*, Brewers Publications, 1989. (9)

G. Fix, "Simplified Quality Control," *Beer and Brewing*, Vol. 10, Brewers Publications, 1990. (24)

G. Fix, "Yeast," *Beer and Brewing*, Vol. 7, Brewers Publications, 1987. (12)

T. Foster, *Pale Ale*, Brewers Publications, 1990. (8)

M. Hennech, *Encyclopedia of Texas Breweries (1836-1918)*, Ale Publications, Irving, Texas, 1990. (19)

M. Jackson, *Pocket Guide to Beer*, Simon and Schuster, 1988. (15)

M. Jackson, *The World Guide to Beer*, The Running Press, Philadelphia, 1988. (17)

D. Miller, *The Complete Handbook of Home Brewing*, Garden Way Publishing, 1988. (22)

D. Miller, *Continental Pilsener*, Brewers Publications, 1990. (10)

D. Miller, "Recipe Formulation," *Beer and Brewing*, Vol. 10, Brewers Publications, 1990. (23)

L. Narziss, "Bottom-fermentation special beers and their characteristics," *Brauwelt International*, 1985. (3)

Nugy, *Brewers Manual*, Jersey Printing, 1948. (6)

K. Oloff and A. Piendl, "Conventional Properties of Several Malt Types," *Brewers Digest*, 1978. (11)

One Hundred Years of Brewing, Arno Press, New York, 1974. (1)

R. Wahl and M. Henius, *American Handy Book of the Brewing, Malting, and Auxiliary Trades*, 2 vols., Wahl Henius Institute of Chicago, 1908. (18)

A. Zimmermann, *Brauereibe briebslehre*, Buffalo, New York, 1904. (2)

HOMEBREWER?

Get the Whole Story!

Join the thousands of American Homebrewers Association® members who read **Zymurgy®** — the magazine for homebrewers and beer lovers.

Every issue of **Zymurgy** is full of tips, techniques, new recipes, new products, equipment and ingredient reviews, beer news, technical articles — the whole world of homebrewing. PLUS, the AHA brings members the National Homebrewers Conference, the National Homebrew Competition, the Beer Judge Certification Program, the Homebrew Club Network, periodic discounts on books from Brewers Publications and much, much more.

MEAD

BOOKS for Brewers and Beer Lovers

Order Now ... Your Brew Will Thank You!

These books offered by Brewers Publications are some of the most sought-after reference tools for homebrewers and professional brewers alike. Filled with tips, techniques, recipes and history, these books will help you expand your brewing horizons. Let the world's foremost brewers help you as you brew. Whatever your brewing level or interest, Brewers Publications has the information necessary for you to brew the best beer in the world — your beer.

Please send me more free information on the following: (check all that apply)

◊ Merchandise and Book Catalog   ◊ Institute for Brewing Studies
◊ American Homebrewers Association®   ◊ Great American Beer Festival®

Ship to:

Name

Address

City   State/Province

Zip/Postal Code   Country

Daytime Phone ( )

Please use this form in conjunction with the standard order form when ordering books from Brewers Publications.

Payment Method

◊ Check or Money Order Enclosed (Payable to Brewers Publications)
◊ Visa   ◊ MasterCard

Card Number   –   –   –   Expiration Date

Name on Card   Signature

Brewers Publications, PO Box 1510, Boulder, CO 80306-1510, USA; (303) 546-6514; Internet orders@aob.org; FAX (303) 447-2825.

MEAD

BREWERS PUBLICATIONS ORDER FORM

PROFESSIONAL BREWING BOOKS

QTY.	TITLE	STOCK #	PRICE	EXT. PRICE
_____	Brewery Planner	500	80.00	_____
_____	North American Brewers Resource Directory	505	80.00	_____
_____	Principles of Brewing Science	463	29.95	_____

THE BREWERY OPERATIONS SERIES
from Micro- and Pubbrewers Conferences

QTY.	TITLE	STOCK #	PRICE	EXT. PRICE
_____	Volume 6, 1989 Conference	536	25.95	_____
_____	Volume 7, 1990 Conference	537	25.95	_____
_____	Volume 8, 1991 Conference, Brewing Under Adversity	538	25.95	_____
_____	Volume 9, 1992 Conference, Quality Brewing — Share the Experience	539	25.95	_____

CLASSIC BEER STYLE SERIES

QTY.	TITLE	STOCK #	PRICE	EXT. PRICE
_____	Pale Ale	401	11.95	_____
_____	Continental Pilsener	402	11.95	_____
_____	Lambic	403	11.95	_____
_____	Vienna, Märzen, Oktoberfest	404	11.95	_____
_____	Porter	405	11.95	_____
_____	Belgian Ale	406	11.95	_____
_____	German Wheat Beer	407	11.95	_____
_____	Scotch Ale	408	11.95	_____
_____	Bock	409	11.95	_____

BEER AND BREWING SERIES, for homebrewers and beer enthusiasts, from National Homebrewers Conference

QTY.	TITLE	STOCK #	PRICE	EXT. PRICE
_____	Volume 8, 1988 Conference	448	21.95	_____
_____	Volume 10, 1990 Conference	450	21.95	_____
_____	Volume 11, 1991 Conference, Brew Free or Die!	451	21.95	_____
_____	Volume 12, 1992 Conference, Just Brew It!	452	21.95	_____

GENERAL BEER AND BREWING INFORMATION

QTY.	TITLE	STOCK #	PRICE	EXT. PRICE
_____	The Art of Cidermaking	468	9.95	_____
_____	Brewing Lager Beer	460	14.95	_____
_____	Brewing Mead	461	11.95	_____
_____	Dictionary of Beer and Brewing	462	19.95	_____
_____	Evaluating Beer	465	19.95	_____
_____	Great American Beer Cookbook	466	24.95	_____
_____	Victory Beer Recipes	467	11.95	_____
_____	Winners Circle	464	11.95	_____

SUBTOTAL _____

Call or write for a free Beer Enthusiast catalog today.
• U.S. funds only.
• All Brewers Publications books come with a money-back guarantee.
* Postage & Handling: $4 for the first book ordered, plus $1 for each book thereafter.
  For Canadian and international orders please add $5 for the first book and $2 for
  each book thereafter. Orders cannot be shipped without appropriate P&H.

Colo. Residents Add
3% Sales Tax _____

P&H * _____

TOTAL _____

Brewers Publications, PO Box 1510, Boulder, CO 80306-1510, USA;
(303) 546-6514; Internet orders@aob.org; FAX (303) 447-2825.

MEAD